# Yes, We Sang!

# Yes, We Sang!
## Songs of the Ghettos and Concentration Camps

SHOSHANA KALISCH

with Barbara Meister

**HARPER & ROW, PUBLISHERS, New York**
Cambridge, Philadelphia, San Francisco, London
Mexico City, São Paulo, Singapore, Sydney

Grateful acknowledgment is made for permission to reprint:

Excerpts from the 1948 CYCO publication of Shmerke Kaczerginski's *Lider fun di Getos un Lagern.* Reprinted by permission of Joseph C. Landis of the Congress for Jewish Culture.

"Tsvey Taybelekh" and "Ziamele" by Ruth Rubin from her collection entitled *Jewish Folksongs* (Oak Publications, 1965). Reprinted by permission of the author and Oak Publications.

"Babi Yar" from *We Are Here* by Chane Mlotek (Workmen's Circle, 1983). Reprinted by permission of the author and the Education Department of the Workmen's Circle.

"Ballad of Crystal Night" and "Nursery Rhyme for Dead Children" by Peter Wortsman. Copyright © 1979 by Peter Wortsman. Reprinted by permission of the author.

Excerpts from *Babi Yar* by A. Anatoli (Kuznetsov), translated by David Floyd. English translation copyright © 1970 by Jonathan Cape Ltd. Reprinted by permission of Farrar, Straus & Giroux, Inc., and Jonathan Cape Ltd.

*To*
*Sisi, Jancsi, Nany,*
*and to*
*Tamara*

# CONTENTS

# ACKNOWLEDGMENTS

I am deeply grateful for Mordechai Sheinkman's piano arrangements, which, far from the routine of the expected, capture fully the soul of the songs.

My heartfelt thanks and gratitude to the following people whose help was vitally instrumental in bringing this book about: Lucy S. Dawidowicz, Ann Harris, Eugen Kalisch, Victor Trasoff, Parks Wightman, and especially John Wykert.

I am also much indebted to the staff of YIVO Institute for Jewish Research in New York for availing their library and archives to me. Special thanks to Dina Abramowicz of the library, who was always knowledgeably around whenever needed. Many thanks to Dr. Mordche Schaechter for reading and correcting the orthography of the Yiddish song texts, which appear at the end of the book.

Since this book originated with my performances of "Songs of the Holocaust," I would like to acknowledge my profound gratitude to Chana and Josef Mlotek and the Workmen's Circle, who first gave me the opportunity to present this program of songs; to Steven Beyer and Sesil Lissberger of the JWB Lecture Bureau, who arranged for performances of my program across the United States; and to Brigitte Muschg, who first brought this program to European audiences.

I also want to thank from my heart all the individuals and friends who in so many different ways were of invaluable help to me in creating and performing this song program: Johanna Bally, Rose Choron, Eiko and Koma, Margaret Falk, Ina Friedman, Dr. Peter Huber, Margrit Keller, Ursa Krattiger, Alex Kulisiewicz, Dr. Ed Levy, Dr. Joel Markowitz, Cath Miodini, Annelise Ott, Pat Pasloff, Naomi Pollack, Lucie and Peter Porges, Michael Posnik, Milton Resnik, Elizabeth Rich, Tova Ronni, Ruth Rubin, Leeny Sack, May Scheff, Martha Schlamme, Abraham Schulman, Hy and Ev Sussman, Milton Taubman, and Isabel Zakin.

Last but not least, thanks to Aaron Asher, my editor at Harper & Row; to his always patient, polite, and helpful assistant, Carol Chen; and to Diane Conley, Linda Dingler, Dan Harvey, Marjorie Horvitz, Katherine Johnson, and Coral Tysliava, whose work on the book is greatly appreciated. Irwin Rabinowitz, perhaps the only music autographer in town with a knowledge of Yiddish, also earns my gratitude.

Extra and special thanks to Julian Bach, my agent, and his staff.

*About the Illustrations*

I would have liked to reproduce pictures of each of the musicians, poets, and singers mentioned, but very few were available. Those few we have been able to include were copied from wilted old snapshots, newspaper clippings, and concert programs. I acknowledge with gratitude the items supplied by the Vilna historian Leyzer Ran, author of the unique three-volume *Jerusalem of Lithuania Illustrated and Documented* (New York, 1974–75). Mr. Ran was also immensely helpful and always graciously available with vital information concerning many details of this book.

Three of the photographs were supplied by YIVO Institute for Jewish Research, New York.

SHOSHANA KALISCH

*New York*
*May 1985*

# Yes, We Sang!

*Nit mayn shuld di troyer-lider,*
*Nit mir iz lib azoy tsu shraybn.*
*Ikh leg avek dem kop a mider,*
*Ongelodn ful mit laydn.*

*Dos veyn-gezang iz nit mayns,*
*S'hot a tsayt gezang geboyrn:*
*Groyse, shvartse, toybe teger*
*Hobn dorkhgekrekhtst dorkh lager-moyern.*

These mournful songs are not my fault,
This is not a style I'd borrow.
Painful thoughts my brain assault,
My head is filled with sorrow.

Not mine these laments full of tears,
They're born of a time which appalls:
Gray, black, deaf days, months, years
Groaned through cold camp walls.

—Poem by Sheva Glaz-Rozenblum
Lodz Ghetto, Auschwitz, and Stutthof

# PROLOGUE

As children, we were taken almost daily to a park lush with old, wild chestnuts, acacias, linden, and other trees, with fragrant flowering bushes and shrubs, with songbirds, with creeping plants that grew over footpaths, and with benches in shady, hidden nooks. There we could lose ourselves for hours, content in the feeling that the world was nothing but a blissful place of hide-and-seek, of grassy hills to roll down, of dandelions in the spring, of frogs or butterflies to chase, of wild chestnuts to be collected in the fall and carved or strung into necklaces.

The park was situated at the edge of Galanta, the small town in southern Czechoslovakia where I was born. In the center of the park stood a castle, a relic of the Austro-Hungarian Empire, to which the town belonged before World War I. The castle had a mysteriously protective quality for us children. A few years later, under Nazi occupation, part of the castle was turned into a prison, where Jews were taken for questioning, torture, and imprisonment, often never to be seen again. During those years I tried to avoid thinking of the park, afraid that I would be reproachful, even bitter, because of the betrayal of its promises. Yet the deep-seated memories of its beauty prevailed and ultimately helped me to sustain the will and hope for my survival.

The poetry and songs created and sung during internment by the Nazis were an even stronger spiritual support to us.

Yes, we sang in the ghettos and concentration camps. Songs were sung even in the death camps. They were the only means of expressing our sadness and grief, defiance and hope. When our spirits sank, the songs took over; they helped us to keep our faith that life held some meaning.

| | |
|---|---|
| *Hier stehst Du* | Here you stand |
| *schweigend* | silent |
| *doch* | yet |
| *wenn Du Dich wendest* | when you turn away |
| *schweige nicht* | do not keep silent |

—Inscription on a memorial monument erected in the former Jewish cemetery in Berlin that was destroyed by the Nazis

My sister Nany and I were confined with one thousand girls and women in Barracks No. 5 of "C" Compound in Birkenau, Auschwitz. This was in 1944, the year we were deported from Galanta. Barracks No. 5 faced the so-called hospital of Birkenau,

1

called *Revier*—sick compound—by the Germans. Patients admitted to the *Revier* were never released. Sooner or later they were carted off to the gas chambers.

Every evening, at roll call in front of our barracks, we saw a black, covered truck pull up in front of the hospital. The back door of the truck was opened and from the hospital a row of selected patients were marched naked into the truck for their last journey. Standing motionless during roll call, I at first closed my eyes, unable to face this sight. Later, I forced myself to watch. I realized that refusing to look would have meant abandoning these human beings during their last hours. And so, every evening at roll call in Auschwitz, with our eyes and hearts we shared the fate of those about to die.

\* \* \*

Survivors are forever puzzled by and in search of the reason for their survival. I marveled at those who soon after the war were able to speak about their lives in the ghettos and concentration camps. I wasn't able to do so; words seemed inadequate. My memories stayed buried within. Meanwhile I studied voice, but I did not make a career of singing. One day in the 1970s—I was then office manager in a marine engineering company in New York—some of the songs we sang in the concentration camp started coming back to me. At first, I would sing these songs to myself. They forced to the surface the mourning I had denied myself for so many years. I had been trying to forget rather than remember my own experience of the Holocaust. As the songs came back, memories and thoughts came with them, and claimed their place in my present life. I left my job and started collecting songs from other survivors. Many songs I found in the archives of various Jewish institutions in New York and abroad.

In 1979, I presented my first public program of "Songs of the Holocaust." I have now sung this program in Europe and throughout the United States. Bringing these songs back to life and recalling the circumstances under which they were created and sung finally gave meaning to my own survival.

The songs in this book are only a few of the many existing songs known to us from that time. Most of those in this collection are expressions of the Jewish experience during the years of Nazi oppression, although I have also included "Moorsoldaten" (Peat Bog Soldiers), the first song known to have been created in a concentration camp, which was written by two non-Jewish prisoners. A song about the fate of Gypsies in the Lodz ghetto and two songs written after World War II, expressing the feelings of the next generation, are also in the book.

To convey what it was like to sing in the ghettos, concentration camps, resistance camps, and hideouts of World War II, I have focused mainly on the events relating to the songs and the people who first sang them. Some of my own experiences are interwoven in the text.

In my research, I came across the story of the singer Liuba Levitska, who performed in the Vilna ghetto. I was inspired by her courage and moved by her tragic life. I have written this book with Liuba Levitska in mind, and in memory of all who created, sang, or listened to poetry and songs in those worst of times.

# DI NAKHT
## The Night

Liuba Levitska, 1917–1943. This photograph was copied from the 1940 program notes of the Lithuanian Jewish Theater's production of Abraham Goldfadn's play *Akeydas Yitskhok* (Isaac's Sacrifice). Liuba sang the part of Isaac in this performance before the German occupation of Vilna.

When Liuba Levitska, the beloved "nightingale" of the Vilna ghetto, sang "Di Nakht" at a concert on January 18, 1942, the ghetto population had already been reduced to a third of its original size. The concert took place just a few weeks after the "night of the *gele shayne*"—yellow papers—when the Germans distributed identification certificates entitling each bearer and up to four members of his family to at least temporary survival. Three thousand such papers were issued for some thirty thousand people. The remaining fifteen thousand Jews were hunted down in three consecutive roundups—*Aktionen*—loaded on trucks, taken to the nearby Ponar woods, and shot.

The concert was controversial, and accounts differ as to who organized it so soon after the massacres. Hermann Kruk, the Vilna ghetto chronicler, criticizes the event in his ghetto diary. "One doesn't play theater in a cemetery," he wrote, urging others to boycott the concert. But it did take place, and it proved a moving and fitting memorial for Vilna's martyrs. "The audience stood in sacred silence as one stands in front of an open grave. Every word, every sound, recalled the victims at Ponar," wrote the poet Abraham Sutskever, describing the event. A choral recitation of Chaim N. Bialik's

"S'g'lust Zikh Mir Vaynen" (I Am Moved to Weep) opened the program, which included cantor Josef Eydlson's singing of "Eli, Eli, Lomo Ozavtoni" (O Lord, Why Hast Thou Abandoned Me); Chopin's "Funeral March"; and "Yisrolik," the first song written on a ghetto theme. Liuba Levitska sang Dina's prison lament from Abraham Goldfadn's opera *Bar-Kochba*, and, among other songs, "Di Nakht."

"Di Nakht" is a Yiddish song written in New York in 1929 by Mikhl Gelbart and Aaron Domnits, Jewish emigrants from Eastern Europe. The song found its way to European Jews before World War II, as did many other Yiddish songs written in America. During the Nazi oppression, when Jews could not express their feelings openly, there was a special significance to songs like "Di Nakht," with its stark, metaphoric forebodings of uncertainty, danger, and ultimate despair. And Liuba Levitska expressed it all with her singing in the Vilna ghetto.

Liuba Levitska was born in 1917 in Vilna, Polish Lithuania. Her great musical potential was recognized while she was still a student at the local conservatory. She continued her vocal and dramatic studies at the Vienna Conservatory, from which she was graduated with honors. Of small build, with a beautiful face and an unusually spirited, cheerful personality, Liuba was universally liked and admired. Her coloratura soprano might have made her internationally known had her career, and then her life, not ended prematurely. In 1938, barely twenty-one years old, she enjoyed her first great success, singing Violetta in *La Traviata* at Vilna's Yiddish Opera Theater. This company, under Sigmund Turkov, produced original works as well as the standard opera repertoire translated into Yiddish. Successful productions of Goldfadn's *Shulamith* and *Bar-Kochba*, in which Liuba sang the fiery Dina, brought her to Warsaw's Yidisher Kunst Teater, the Jewish Art Theater. An extended run was interrupted by Hitler's invasion of Poland in 1939. This ended the only idyllic period of Liuba's brief life.

Liuba returned to Vilna to be with her family. At the beginning of the war, while the Russians occupied Vilna, her career continued. She sang on the radio, taught a class at the conservatory, and was invited to concertize in Moscow. But the trip to Russia never materialized, for in June of 1940, the Germans took Vilna and the Jews were herded into the ghetto.

Liuba might have remained in hiding outside the ghetto, thanks to some non-Jewish musician friends who offered her sanctuary, but her mother was trapped inside, and she chose to join her. Each day Liuba was marched with a small group assigned to hard labor outside the ghetto. Upon her return from the exhausting work, she taught singing to a class of children at the ghetto's improvised music school.

When Liuba sang "Di Nakht" for the stunned mourners of the Vilna ghetto, she had already survived beatings, deprivations, and humiliations. Her ability to sing in the face of the dehumanizing daily practices of the Nazis was a unique form of resistance which gave solace and courage to those around her. Her voice was silenced only by her death at Ponar in 1943.

# DI NAKHT
## The Night

Words by Aaron Domnits

Music by Mikhl Gelbart

S'iz key - ner mit mir in der
*There's no one with me in the*

nakht,
*night,*
Di nakht nor a-leyn iz mit mir.
*— Dark-ness a-lone is with me.*
Oyf
*On*

ve - gn far-khmu - ret un shtum,
*roads ob-scured by dark - ness dense,*
Di
*—*

shtil - keyt a-leyn van-dert um.
*Hol-low still-ness all that I can sense.*

Ikh gey, s'iz a vay - ter der
*I go;___ long is my*

veg,___
*way,___*

Far - vol - knt un toyb iz di nakht.
*The cloud - ed night does not___ hear.*

Vu - hin,___ vu - hin,___
*Where?___ Where?___*

Freg dem ri - tm fun di trit.
*Ask the rhy-thm of your steps.*

Zey gi - bn keyn ent - fer mir nit. S'iz
*No an - swer comes to my ear. There's*

6

S'iz keyner mit mir in der nakht,
Di nakht nor aleyn iz mit mir.
Oyf vegn farkhmuret un shtum,
Di shtilkeyt aleyn vandert um.

Ikh gey, s'iz a vayter der veg,
Farvolknt un toyb iz di nakht.
Vuhin, vuhin, freg dem ritm fun di trit.
Zey gibn keyn entfer mir nit.

S'iz keyner mit mir in der nakht;
Di nakht nor aleyn iz mit mir.
Vos vayter un vayter ahin—
Vuhin, shtile vegn, vuhin?

*There's no one with me in the night,*
*Darkness alone is with me.*
*On roads obscured by darkness dense,*
*Hollow stillness all that I can sense—*

*I go: long is my way,*
*The clouded night does not hear.*
*Where? Where? Ask the rhythm of your steps.*
*No answer comes to my ear.*

*There's no one with me in the night;*
*Darkness alone is with me.*
*On and on in lonely despair—*
*But where, silent roads, where?*

# TSVEY TAYBELEKH
## Two Doves

"Tsvey Taybelekh," an old Yiddish folk song made popular in the Vilna ghetto by Liuba Levitska, tells of two loving doves torn from one another by an unknown evil force. To the Jews, who could not openly express their feelings of pain and sorrow, the tragic fate of the doves in this plaintive song symbolized their own tragedies—the shattering of families by the Nazis, who drove thousands away across the ocean, imprisoned countless others, and destroyed love and happiness.

The concluding lines of the song—

A curse on that person—so evil, so cruel—
Who so soon destroyed my own true love

—are a barely concealed expression of the anger the Jews felt toward their oppressors.

Liuba's interpretation of this song was so intense that her listeners made her sing it every time she performed, and thus "Tsvey Taybelekh" was one of the most popular songs in the Vilna ghetto.

Liuba's life in the ghetto was full of trials. During one of the roundups, when Jews were hunted down to be shot at Ponar, Liuba hid for two days under the refuse in a covered garbage can; at another roundup, she was caught hiding and thrown into the ghetto's dreaded Lukiszki Prison, where she was tortured by SS police officer Horst Schweinenberg, who stabbed her repeatedly with his sword. Miraculously, Liuba survived. After several weeks in the ghetto hospital, she had recovered sufficient strength to resume teaching in the clandestine music school and to sing again at the concerts.

In January 1943, about a year after the first concert in memory of those massacred in Ponar, Liuba was rehearsing with the ghetto orchestra, under the direction of Wolf Durmashkin, for an opera performance in which she was to sing the leading role. She practiced her part each day, softly singing it to herself as she marched to and from her work. On the day of the performance, though exhausted from ten hours of scrubbing military barracks, she returned to the ghetto filled with anticipation of the evening's performance. She was also apprehensive, for she concealed beneath her clothes a small bag of food that a non-Jewish friend had smuggled to her, which she looked forward to bringing to her ailing mother. At the gate, Franz Mürer, the SS commander of the ghetto, had Liuba's group searched. When the contraband was found on her, she was punished with twenty-five lashes on her naked body and was imprisoned in the ghetto's prison tower.

There was no opera performance that night. For a month, Liuba was kept in solitary confinement. There, too, she sang, to comfort prisoners in adjacent cells, most of whom had been condemned to death. "Liuba is singing in the tower," said the people of the ghetto. The nightingale of the ghetto had become the songbird of the prison tower. Even the SS guards would come to her cell door to hear her beautiful singing.

Meanwhile the Jewish ghetto authorities exerted all efforts with the SS to have Liuba released, but Mürer and his adjutant, Martin Weiss, the Ponar henchman, decided differently. One day Weiss himself drove Liuba to Ponar in his car, his Gestapo girlfriend Hilde Degner, a former university student from Hamburg, at his side. At the killing ground, Degner ordered Liuba to remove her clothes—as all those condemned to death were forced to do on their way to the ditches into which they fell when shot. When Liuba at first did not obey, Degner threatened to pierce her eyes, a surefire method she had learned from Weiss. She then shot Liuba several times.

Though death was all too commonplace an occurrence in the ghetto, the entire community was shaken at the news of her murder. Liuba's voice, which had brought memories and dreams of a happier time, was silenced. Details of her last moments became legendary among the ghetto people. It was said that she sang all the way through Vilna on the drive to Ponar, and kept on singing as she was led to the pile of bodies on which she was to die. The song she sang as she was shot was "Tsvey Taybelekh."

# TSVEY TAYBELEKH
## Two Doves

Author unknown
After an old Yiddish love song

Slow (♩=48)

Tsvey
Two

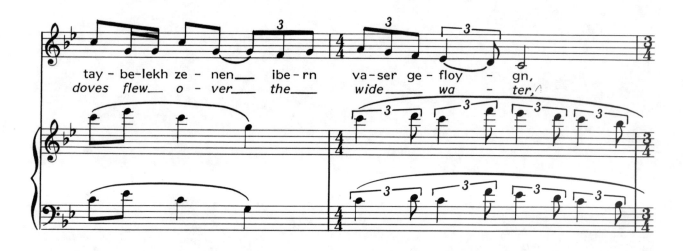

tay - be - lekh ze - nen___ ibe - rn va - ser ge - floy___ gn,
*doves flew___ o - ver___ the___ wide___ wa - ter,*

In di pis - ke - lekh ho - bn zey zikh ge - kisht. Far-
*Their___ lov - ing beaks kissing___ high a - bove. A*

10

shol - tn zol ve - rn___ ye - ner mentsh oyf der velt,___
*curse on that per - son___ so___ e - vil, so cruel___*

Vos er hot zikh in un - dzer li - be___ oy, a - rayn - ge - misht.
*Who___ tore___ from___ me___ my___ own true love.*

**Fine**

Vos er hot un - dzer li - be___ a - zoy gikh tsu - sheydt.
*Who so soon___ de - stroyed___ our___ own true love.*

11

Tsvey taybelekh zenen ibern vaser gefloygn,
In di piskelekh hobn zey zikh gekisht.
Farsholtn zol vern yener mentsh oyf der velt,
Vos er hot zikh in undzer libe—oy, arayngemisht.

Un az du vest kumen in a vaytn land, lubelyu,
In mayne verter zolstu zikh badenken.
Un az du vest kumen iber a tifn vaser, lubelyu,
Far groys tsores zolstu zikh nit dertrenken.

Un az du vest kumen in a fremdn land, lubelyu,
Mayne verter zolstu bakenen.
Un az du vest kumen iber a groysn fayer, lubelyu,
Far groys tsores zolstu zikh nit farbrenen.

Tsvey taybelekh zenen ibern vaser gefloygn,
Zeyere fligelekh hobn zey tsushpreyt.
Farsholtn zol vern yener mentsh oyf der velt,
Vos er hot undzer libe, azoy gikh tsusheydt.

*Two doves flew over the wide water,*
*Their loving beaks kissing high above.*
*A curse on that person—so evil, so cruel—*
*Who tore from me my own true love.*

*And when you have come to a far-off land, lubelyu,*
*Be sure to remember my words of love.*
*And when you have come to deep waters, lubelyu,*
*Do not drown for sorrow, my little dove.*

*And when you have come to a distant land, lubelyu,*
*Be sure to remember my words of love.*
*And should you come across a great fire, lubelyu,*
*Do not burn for sorrow, my little dove.*

*Two doves flew over the wide water,*
*Spreading their wings high above.*
*A curse on that person—so evil, so cruel—*
*Who so soon destroyed our own true love.*

# S'BRENT
## It Burns!

Mordekhai Gebirtig, 1887–1942.

Mordekhai Gebirtig, a much-loved Yiddish folk poet, wrote "S'brent" (also known as "Dos Shtetl Brent"—The Little Town's Afire) one year before the outbreak of World War II. It was his reaction to the series of bloody riots against Polish Jews that culminated in a pogrom in the little town of Przytik in central Poland. During the pogrom, in which three Jews were killed and sixty more wounded—a small pogrom by later standards—one Jew killed a Polish attacker in self-defense. He was condemned at a trial in which no distinction was made between attackers and defenders.

"S'brent" was a dramatic warning of disaster. Scarcely noticed at the time, the powerful visionary character of the song was realized only after the German invasion in 1939, when the world around Europe's Jews was literally burning.

Mordekhai Gebirtig had been celebrated for his poems and songs about Jewish life in prewar Poland. He was "the gentle harp of the Polish Jew," as Yisoskhor Fater calls him in his book *Jewish Music in Poland*, praising the sensitivity and compassion with which Gebirtig portrayed his people in his works.

Krakow, the birthplace of Gebirtig, is a city on the Vistula River in Galitsia, south Poland. Before World War II, Krakow had been one of Europe's most important Jewish settlements, with a history that could be traced back to the fourteenth century. Gebirtig grew up in this community rich in social and cultural activities. His talent and love for music were manifested early—as a small child he taught himself to play the shepherd's flute. There was no money for his education, and to earn his keep he worked in his brother-in-law's furniture store. He sought spiritual nourishment through the Jewish working people's cultural circles, which he joined as a youth. Soon he met the writer Abraham Reizin, and under his influence began writing verse and songs.

Gebirtig's first book of poetry, *Folkstimlekh* (In a Folk Mode), was published in 1920. In 1936, on the thirtieth anniversary of the beginning of his literary career, his friends surprised him with a publication of his poetry entitled *Mayne Lider* (My Songs). Menakhem Kipnis, an important critic and folklorist of the time, wrote, "Gebirtig is the perfect Jewish folk poet."

In the true tradition of the folk poet, Gebirtig turned many of his poems into songs and sang them himself. Though not a schooled musician, he created the most beloved songs of the Yiddish song literature.

During the First World War, Gebirtig served in the Austro-Hungarian army. Thrown into daily contact with Czechs, Hungarians, Serbo-Croatians, and Rumanians, he eagerly absorbed their richly varied folk melodies. Elements of this music are blended in his colorful songs, which were sung by everyone, including wandering street musicians, who performed them throughout Poland. His songs, which treat the timeless themes of love, childhood, marriage, old age, as well as the particular struggles and joys of Polish-Jewish life, are suffused with his wisdom and wit. Some of his songs, like "Dray Tekhterl" (Three Daughters), which tells of the pleasures and difficulties of raising children and then losing them, are about his own family. Many describe the struggles of the poor. His song about a pickpocket, "Avreml der Marvikher," creates sympathy even for this low-life character.

"S'brent," written in 1938, anticipates the tragic epoch that followed. *Shtetl*, a diminutive of *shtot*, the Yiddish word for "town," meant more than just "small town" to the Polish Jews. It represented a unique way of life centered around family, synagogue, and marketplace, focused on *yiddishkeit* (Jewishness) and *menshlikhkeit* (humaneness). Characterized by struggle and more often than not by great poverty, the shtetl was nonetheless a colorful world full of music and love of life.

At the time Gebirtig wrote "S'brent," he sensed the end of the shtetl era and of Jewish life in Poland—a premonition that was realized during the Nazi occupation. His song was, and still is, a warning of the dangers of passivity in the face of oppression.

# S'BRENT

## It Burns!

Mordekhai Gebirtig

S' - brent,__ bri - der - lekh,
*It burns,__ broth-ers dear, it*

s' - brent! (Oy,) Un-dzer o - rem shte - tl ne-bekh brent!__
*burns!___ Our poor lit - tle shte - tl is on fire!___*

Bey - ze vin - tn mit yir - go - zn Ray - sn, bre - khn un tse - blo - zn,
*Fu - ri - ous - ly an - gry winds storm, Mad - ly a - round the whipped flames swarm,*

Refrain

Shtar-ker nokh di vil - de fla - men, Alts a - rum shoyn brent. Un ir shteyt un
*Ev - er wild-er grows the fierce blaze, Ev-'ry-thing's on fire! And you stand a-*

kukt a - zoy zikh Mit far - leyg - te hent. Un ir shteyt un
*round and stare___ While the___ flames grow higher. And you stand a-*

Fine

kukt a - zoy zikh___ Un-dzer shte - tl s' - brent!
*round and stare___ While our shte - tl burns.___*

S'brent, briderlekh, s'brent!
Oy, undzer orem shtetl nebekh brent!
Beyze vintn mit yirgozn
Raysn, brekhn un tseblozn,
Shtarker nokh di vilde flamen—
Alts arum shoyn brent.

Refrain
Un ir shteyt un kukt azoy zikh
Mit farleygte hent.
Un ir shteyt un kukt azoy zikh
Undzer shtetl brent!

S'brent, briderlekh, s'brent!
Oy, undzer orem shtetl nebekh brent
S'hobn shoyn di fayertsungen
Dos gantse shtetl ayngeshlungen—
Un di beyze vintn huzhen,
Undzer shtetl brent!

(Refrain)

S'brent, briderlekh, s'brent!
Oy, es ken kholile kumen der moment:
Undzer shtot mit undz tsuzamen
Zol oyf ash avek in flamen,
Blaybn zol—vi nokh a shlakht,
Nor puste, shvartse vent!

(Refrain)

S'brent, briderlekh, s'brent!
Di hilf iz nor in aykh aleyn gevendt.
Oyb dos shtetl iz aykh tayer,
Nemt di keylim, lesht dos fayer,
Lesht mit ayer eygn blut,
Bavayzt, az ir dos kent.

Refrain
Shteyt nit, brider, ot azoy zikh
Mit farleygte hent.
Shteyt nit brider, lesht dos fayer
Undzer shtetl brent!

It burns, brothers dear, it burns!
Our poor little shtetl is on fire!
Furiously angry winds storm,
Madly around the whipped flames swarm,
Ever wilder grows the fierce blaze—
Everything's on fire!

Refrain
And you stand around and stare
While the flames grow higher.
And you stand around and stare
While our shtetl burns.

It burns, brothers dear, it burns!
Our poor little shtetl is on fire.
Tongues of fire have swallowed down
Houses, streets, our whole little town,
And the angry winds are howling—
Our shtetl is on fire.

(Refrain)

It burns, brothers dear, it burns!
Our little shtetl soon will be on fire.
This our village in which we dwell
Will be a fiery hell,
Blackened as after a battle,
Walls like a burning pyre.

(Refrain)

It burns, brothers dear, it burns!
If we don't help ourselves, our fate is dire.
If you love your poor little town,
Please don't let them burn it all down.
Put out the flames with your own blood—
Only you can squelch the fire.

Refrain
Brothers, don't just stand and stare
While the flames grow higher.
Brothers, don't just stand and stare
While our shtetl burns.

# MINUTN FUN BITOKHN
## Moments of Confidence

In Krakow, as everywhere else in Poland, Jews were subjected to terror and death as soon as the Germans invaded in September 1939. Their homes were looted, their temples and schools destroyed; they were dragged into the streets, beaten, abused. In spite of these humiliations, they could not at first conceive of the inhumanity with which the Germans were to proceed toward total annihilation.

The poems written by Mordekhai Gebirtig at the beginning of the Nazi occupation were still dominated by the gentle tone for which he had been known. They expressed belief that despite the hardships Jews might be forced to bear, justice and goodness would ultimately prevail. One of his poems of that time, however, "S'tut Vey" (It Hurts), expresses Gebirtig's pain over "Poland's sons and daughters," who took pleasure in joining the Germans in the humiliation of the Jews, with whom the Poles had been friends just yesterday.

Most of the Jews were expelled from Krakow in the first year of the war and had to settle in small villages nearby. Gebirtig and his family moved to nearby Lagievniki, where they lived in cramped quarters with other families. Food was scarce and life squalid. Early in 1942, the Germans ordered all the Jews who had been dispersed into surrounding villages back to Krakow and into a ghetto. Gebirtig, at that time sixty years old, was reunited in the ghetto with two friends, Abraham Neyman, a painter, and the musician Julius Hofman. The artists found solace in one another, absorbing themselves in creative work, which helped them to bear the oppressive ghetto life. Despite the devastating conditions, Gebirtig's poems of that time still show awareness of "spring, field, sunshine, and forest." But in a poem dedicated to one of his three daughters, he writes:

| | |
|---|---|
| *Kh'hob shoyn lang, shoyn zeyer lang,* | It has been a long, long time |
| *Nit gehert keyn fidl-klang. . . .* | Since I have heard fiddle music. . . . |
| | |
| *S'veynen felder, s'veynt der vald,* | Fields and forests are weeping |
| *Nokh yetvedn mentshn vos falt. . . .* | For each and every man who fell. . . . |

To fight the bitterness growing within him and to boost the morale of the Jews in the ghetto, Gebirtig wrote "Minutn fun Bitokhn" (Moments of Confidence), a song inspired by the fervent spirit of Khassidic melodies. In the second of the verses, Gebirtig compares his own era to that of Haman, who, under King Ahasuerus (Xerxes I, 486–465 B.C.), according to the Book of Esther, planned the death of all Jews in Persia. Ultimately Haman was hung instead on the very gallows he had prepared for Mordekhai the Jew. In the third and fourth stanzas he angrily alludes to one of the frequent humiliating tasks the Jews were subjected to by the invading Germans: the sweeping and scrubbing of streets and public places, to the abuses of jeering onlookers.

Gebirtig not only tried to instill with his song the courage to prevail but also aimed at awakening defiance and contempt toward the oppressors. Thus "Minutn fun Bitokhn" planted the seeds of resistance in ghetto youth.

Beginning in January 1943, thousands of Jews were deported daily from the Krakow ghetto, a process that continued until its total liquidation. Overcome by anger and sorrow, Gebirtig wrote:

| | |
|---|---|
| *Nekome far undzer laydn un payn,* | Revenge for our suffering and pain, |
| *Far—mames, yesoymes, almones—* | For mothers, orphans, and widows— |
| *Nekome, vet shrayen aroys fun der erd* | Revenge, will the earth cry from under |
| *Dos blut fun milionen korbones!* | For the blood of millions of victims! |

In May 1943, Gebirtig wrote his last and perhaps his saddest poem. With it, he turned to biting sarcasm, something totally alien to his nature. Its cynical verses mock the blind faith Jews evince even when facing death:

| | |
|---|---|
| *S'iz gut, s'iz gut, s'iz gut.* | It's good, it's good, it's good. |
| *Di Yidelekh shrayen: S'iz gut!* | The Jews shout: It's good! |
| *Der soyne der vilder* | The wild enemy |
| *Geyt groyzam un shnel,* | Goes horribly and fast, |
| *Un vi nor er kumt, vert* | And wherever he comes, |
| *Fun lebn a tel.* | Life becomes death. |
| *Un Yidelekh shrayen: S'iz gut,* | And the Jews shout: It's good, |
| *S'iz voyl, s'iz fayn,* | And the Jews are content. It's good, |
| *S'ken beser nit zayn.* | It's all right, it's fine, |
| | It couldn't be better. |

It took the horrors of Nazi oppression to change the "gentle harp" into a bitter voice of rebellion.

On June 4, 1943, known in Krakow as Bloody Thursday, the Nazis surrounded the ghetto and marched the Jews to waiting cattle cars. To speed up the procession, the Germans struck the weary marchers with their rifle butts. Anyone who could not move fast enough was shot.

Among the first victims were Mordekhai Gebirtig and his friend the painter Abraham Neyman. They were hit almost simultaneously and died under the feet of those who were able to continue to the freight train headed for Belzets, an extermination camp.

# MINUTN FUN BITOKHN
## Moments of Confidence

Mordekhai Gebirtig

Fast (♩=132)

Yi – dn, zol zayn frey – lekh!__ Shoyn nit lang,__ ikh hof.
*Jews, be mer – ry, be__ strong!__ Don't give up,__ but__ hope. The*

S'ekht bald di mil – kho – me, Es kumt bald zey – er sof.
*war will soon be o – ver And they will soon be gone. Be*

20

Frey - lekh, nor nit zor - gn, Un nit a - rum - geyn trib.
*mer - ry, and no griev - ing, Don't give in to de - spair. There's*

Hot ge - duld, bi - to - khn Un nemt alts on far lib. Un
*com - fort in be - liev - ing, Have pa - tience to for - bear. Have*

nemt alts on far lib. Ay - day, Hot bi - to - khn,
*pa - tience to for - bear. There's com - fort in be - liev - ing, have*

Nemt alts on far lib. Ay - day, Hot bi - to - khn,
*pa - tience to for - bear. There's com - fort in be - liev - ing, have*

Nemt alts on far lib.
*pa-tience to for-bear.*

ho - bn zey in d'rerd!___
*Hench-men, go to hell!___*

Yidn, zol zayn freylekh!
Shoyn nit lang, ikh hof:
S'ekht bald di milkhome,
Es kumt bald zeyer sof.
Freylekh, nor nit zorgn,
Un nit arumgeyn trib.
Hot geduld, bitokhn—
Un nemt alts on far lib.

Nor geduld, bitokhn,
Nit lozt aroys fun hant.
Undzer alt kley-zayin,
Vos halt undz gor banand.
Hulyet, tantst talyonim.
Shoyn nit lang, ikh hof—
Geven amol a Homen,
Es vart oyf im zayn sof.

Hulyet, tantst talyonim.
Laydn ken a yid.
S'vet di shverste arbet,
Undz keynmol makhn mid.
Kern? Zol zayn kern!
Kol-zman ir vet zeyn
Iz umzist dos kern,
S'vet do nit vern reyn.

Vashn? Zol zayn vashn!
Kayins royter flek,
Hevls blut fun hartsn—
Dos vasht zikh nit avek.
Traybt undz fun di dires,
Shnaydt undz op di berd.
Yidn, zol zayn freylekh!
Mir hobn zey in d'rerd!

*Jews, be merry, be strong!*
*Don't give up, but hope:*
*The war will soon be over*
*And they will soon be gone.*
*Be merry, and no grieving,*
*Don't give in to despair.*
*There's comfort in believing—*
*Have patience to forbear.*

*Have patience, have confidence,*
*Hold them close at hand.*
*Our spirit is our weapon*
*To keep us a tight-knit band.*
*Dance, ye wicked henchmen.*
*Before long, you'll see—*
*Like Haman long before you,*
*Dire your end will be.*

*Dance, ye wicked henchmen.*
*We Jews have known travail.*
*Despite the cruelest labor,*
*Our strength will yet prevail.*
*Must we sweep? Then we'll sweep!*
*As long as need be.*
*But no amount of sweeping*
*Will clean your infamy.*

*Blood that flowed from Abel*
*Makes a dark-red stain—*
*No amount of scrubbing*
*Can cleanse the hands of Cain.*
*You can drive us from our houses,*
*Cut our beards, our joys dispel.*
*Jews, be gay, be merry!*
*Henchmen, go to hell!*

# BABI YAR

Babi Yar, the "Old Wives' Ravine," was a bucolic recreational area on the outskirts of Kiev, the capital of the Ukraine. In September 1941, just ten days after the German troops occupied Kiev, 33,771 Jews were murdered there on two consecutive days. The appalling massacres were committed by the Germans under the supervision of two SS men, Paul Radomski and Wilhelm Rieder, with the willing help of some of the Ukrainian police.

At dawn on September 29 and 30, Kiev's Jews, young and old, men, women, and children, were led in long processions through the town and along the cemetery to the big ravine at Babi Yar. There they were forced to strip, prodded by blows from rifle butts and rubber truncheons. Their bodies streaked with blood, the Jews then had to stand at the edge of the ravine; as they were machine-gunned, they fell into the pit below. To save bullets, the Germans threw many of the small children into the pits alive. The air was filled with the screams of the victims—many of whom went insane during the process—the sound of machine-gun fire, the barking of dogs trained to bite those trying to escape. The Germans played dance tunes at full volume on a sound system to drown out the infernal noise, but it could still be heard in the neighboring villages.

During their twenty-seven-month occupation of Kiev, the Germans murdered about 51,000 Jews at Babi Yar. A very few, who were just injured, survived the massacres by crawling out at night from under the pile of bodies and the sand that had been shoveled on top of them.

Time is needed to absorb tragic events. Even more time is necessary to transmute shattering experiences into artistic expression. Thus the song that evokes the horrors of Babi Yar was conceived a decade after the massacres.

The song "Babi Yar" was written in 1951 in Moscow by the Russian-Jewish poet Shike Driz and the musician Rivka Boyarska. Shike Driz, born in the Ukraine in 1908, studied sculpture at the Kiev Art Institute. His talent for poetry and storytelling emerged later. In his younger years he was best known for his children's poems in both Yiddish and Russian. During World War II, a soldier stationed in Galitsia, on the border between Russia and German-occupied Poland, he was able to help many Polish Jews to escape. After the war, having settled in Moscow, he worked as a writer. He met Rivka Boyarska, with whom he established a close artistic collaboration.

Boyarska, too, had written many songs for children. Since she was primarily regarded as an educator, her compositions were not much appreciated until folklorist

Z. Kiselhof discovered her talent. Her works began to be published and performed.

Boyarska's husband, Jehoshua Lubomirski, recalls in his memoirs how "Babi Yar" was written. One evening, Boyarska played and sang four of her lullabies to their friend Shike Driz. She then talked about a friend whose two small children had been buried alive at Babi Yar. Driz listened intently and, wordlessly, went home. He returned the next day and told Boyarska that, unable to sleep because of her moving songs and the account of the Babi Yar mother, he had written a poem. Boyarska, deeply touched by the tragic poem, started to set it to music. Its contents oppressed her so that she frequently burst into tears and had to stop working.

Boyarska finished the song in three days. When she and Driz sang it together for the first time, their voices fused in a cry of lament.

"Babi Yar" became well known almost immediately. It was orchestrated by the conductor Nathan Rakhlin and was often performed by the singer Nechetskaya. In 1969, the verses were published in Moscow in a book of Yiddish poetry by Driz entitled *Di Firte Strune* (The Fourth String). In place of the refrain of the song version, "Lyulinke-lu-lu," the poem ends with the following lines:

> *Mit dernen un mit kropeve, farvaksn zaynen stezhkes*
> *Fun shtile, vayse toybn gevorn holovezhkes.*
> *Keyn tsvaygl nit keyn bletl fun dem demb dem hoyln—*
> *Geblibn iz a bergele, fliendike koyln.*

> With thorns and weeds are the paths overgrown,
> Quiet white doves became burnt-out logs.
> Not a little branch nor a leaf on the hollow oak—
> What's left is a heap of coal dust.

Before the Germans retreated from Kiev toward the end of the war, they tried to conceal the massacres of Babi Yar by exhuming the bodies, burning them, and leveling the ground. The "coal dust" in the last line of the poem is in fact the ashes of burnt bones which cover the whole area around Babi Yar—a vast surface of gray sand.

No official recognition of the mass murders at Babi Yar had been given by the Russians after the war until Yevgeny Yevtushenko gained worldwide attention with his poem "Babi Yar," which begins: "No monument stands over Babi Yar."

Yevtushenko continues:

> And I myself
> am one massive, soundless scream
> above the thousand thousand buried here.

> I am
> each old man
> here shot dead.

> I am
> every child here shot dead.

In 1962, Dmitri Shostakovich integrated Yevtushenko's poem into his masterful thirteenth symphony, "Babi Yar," scored for orchestra, voice, and choir.

In 1976, a monument to those who were massacred was finally built on the site of their martyrdom.

# BABI YAR

Words by Shike Driz

Music by Rivka Boyarska

Slow, mournful (♩=44)

Volt ikh oyf-ge-han-gen dos vi-gl oyf a bal - kn, Un ge-
*I would like to hang the___ ba-by's cra-dle from___ a beam, And___*

hoy-det, ge-hoy-det mayn yin-ge-le, mayn Yan-kl. Iz di shtub ant-ru-nen
*rock my lit-tle boy, my lit-tle Yan-kl, to his dream.___ But the house has dis-ap-*

mit a flam___ fa - yer___ Vi zhe kon ikh hoy - den mayn
*peared in flame and fire,___ How can I rock my lit - tle Yan - kl,*

yin-ge-le, mayn ta-yern. Ah,___ Ah.___
*my___ hearts de-sire?___ Ah,___ Ah.___*

1.2.3.

Volt ikh
*I would*

4.

Helft mir, ma - mes, helft mir oys - klo-gn dem ni - gn___
*Help me, moth-ers, help me, mourn with me and weep___*

Helft mir, ma-mes, helft mir dem Ba — bi Yar oyf-vi – gn. Ah,_____
*Help me, moth-ers, help me rock the Ba – bi Yar to sleep!___ Ah,_____*

Ah,_____
*Ah,_____*

Lu-lin-ke lu lu,___ lu-lin-ke lu-lu.___ Ah,_____
*Lu-lin-ke lu lu,___ lu-lin-ke lu-lu.___ Ah,_____*

Lu-lin-ke lu lu,___ Ah._____ lu-lin-ke lu-lu.___
*Lu-lin-ke lu lu,___ Ah._____ lu-lin-ke lu-lu.___*

Volt ikh oyfgehangen dos vigl oyf a balkn,
Un gehoydet, gehoydet mayn yingele, mayn Yankl.
Iz di shtub antrunen mit a flam fayer—
Vi zhe kon ikh hoyden mayn yingele, mayn tayern?
Ah, ah, ah...

Volt ikh oyfgehangen dos vigl oyf a beyml,
Un gehoydet, gehoydet mayn yingele, mayn Shleyml.
Iz mir nit geblibn keyn fodem fun keyn tsikh.
Iz mir nit geblibn keyn bendl fun keyn shikh.
Ah, ah, ah...

Volt ikh opgeshorn di tsep mayne, di lange,
Un oyf zey dos vigl, dos vigl oyfgehangen.
Veys ikh nit, vu zukht men di beyndelekh atsinder,
Di beyndelekh, di tayere, fun beyde mayne kinder.
Ah, ah, ah...

Helft mir, mames, helft mir oysklogn mayn nign.
Helft mir, mames, helft mir dem Babi Yar farvign.
Ah, ah, ah...
Lyulinke-lu-lu...

*I would like to hang the baby's cradle from a beam,*
*And rock my little boy, my little Yankl, to his dream.*
*But the house has disappeared in flame and fire—*
*How can I rock my little Yankl, my heart's desire?*
*Ah, ah, ah...*

*I would like to hang the baby's cradle from a tree,*
*And rock and rock my little boy, my dear Shloyme.*
*But there's nothing left—not even a scrap or shred.*
*But there's nothing left—not even a shoelace,*
  *not a single thread.*
*Ah, ah, ah...*

*I would like to cut my braids, so black, so long,*
*And swing the cradle on them, the whole night long.*
*But I don't know where to find the little bones,*
*The bones of my darlings, my precious little ones.*
*Ah, ah, ah...*

*Help me, mothers, help me, mourn with me and weep.*
*Help me, mothers, help me rock the Babi Yar to sleep.*
*Ah, ah, ah...*
*Lyulinke-lu-lu...*

# THE BALLAD
# OF CRYSTAL NIGHT

Immediately after Hitler came to power in Germany in 1933, severe restrictive measures against the Jews eliminated them from all levels of social, economic, professional, and public life. The Gestapo arrested Jews daily under the pretext of slanderous accusations. In addition, vicious brainwashing in schools, universities, and the media systematically prepared the German people for a collective anti-Semitic outburst. The assassination of a German diplomat in Paris by Hershel Grynszpan, a young Polish Jew, provided the excuse for such an attack. Grynszpan had acted in despair over the deportation of his parents from Germany.

In reprisal, on November 9, 1938, German mobs destroyed Jewish establishments, shops, and homes, set synagogues across the country afire, and made bonfires of books by Jewish and other anti-Nazi authors. Scores of Jews were killed or injured that night, thousands more arrested and shipped to concentration camps.

This first well-organized German pogrom, called Kristallnacht—Crystal Night— because of the broken glass of synagogue and Jewish store windows strewn all over Germany's streets, marked the beginning of the legally sanctioned physical destruction of the German Jews. For the damages caused by the German mobs on Kristallnacht, the Jewish community was fined one million marks. Soon the confiscation of all Jewish property followed, and the mass deportation of German Jews began.

"The Ballad of Crystal Night" relates the events of Kristallnacht. The song was written many years after the war by Peter Wortsman, the son of Viennese Jews who fled Austria when the Nazis took over that country in 1938. Wortsman was born and raised in New York City and studied German folklore as a Fulbright scholar in Europe after he had completed his studies of English and American literature at Brandeis University. He was curious about and eventually deeply involved in the subject of the Holocaust. At the age of twenty-one, he received a fellowship from the Thomas J. Watson Foundation for the interviewing of survivors of Nazi concentration camps in Germany and Poland. Following his research, he wrote a number of stories and songs, including "The Ballad of Crystal Night."

The song describes how the greater part of Germany's population, including the educated, turned into a dehumanized mob of hate and destruction. It also expresses concern over indifference, even callousness, toward these events of only a generation ago, and the fear that no one seems to learn from the past: "Seems there's no way to feel the pain/Till it's your own face that's burned ..."

29

There are two musical versions of this ballad, one of them by Wortsman; the other I wrote.

When I read the text of the song, the tune virtually composed itself in my mind. Born in Czechoslovakia, where the cultural orientation of Jews was strongly influenced by German Judaism, I had developed a very strong identification with the fate of German Jewry. German was the language of the educated Czechoslovakian Jew, who tried to combine secular knowledge and education with Eastern European Jewish religious practices. My father, a pious Orthodox Jew, sincerely devoted to the old rituals, was also an informed, worldly, educated businessman. Along with the hundreds of sacred books in our home, the s'forim and gemores, there was also the encyclopedia of Jewish history by Heinrich Graetz, a modern German Jew. On our bookshelves were treasures of Jewish literature by authors such as Peretz and Shalom Aleichem, as well as works by Goethe and Schiller and other classics of world literature. While my brothers studied the Talmud at the Talmud Torah and my sisters and I were taught Yiddish and Hebrew in the Beth Jacob School, at home we were cared for by an ever-present German nanny, who taught us proper German. Her folk songs mingled with the Yiddish songs my mother sang to us, and as a small child I absorbed them all with great love.

The pain of the German Jews depicted in the text of Peter Wortsman's "Ballad of Crystal Night" was experienced by Jews of other Nazi-occupied countries as well. There, too, neighbors' doors were locked when help was needed and former friends looked away as atrocities were committed.

# THE BALLAD OF CRYSTAL NIGHT

Words by Peter Wortsman

Music by Shoshana Kalisch

My folks came from Vi- en - na For - ty years a - go. Said it was a cul - tured town— Where did all the cul - ture go?

31

pain    Till  it's your own face that's burned;    Till  it's your own face  that's

burned.        Too  late    to  make    a-mends,  my  friends,        Too

late,        my  sto - ry  ends.____

My folks came from Vienna
Forty years ago,
Said it was a cultured town—
Where'd all the culture go?
I only heard the echo.
I don't know.

Oh, the fine old-fashioned doctors
Knew all there was to learn:
The same men could recite their Greek
And watch the fires burn,
Burn, and thank God
It's not their turn.

'Twas the ninth night of November
Nineteen thirty-eight:
Skies aglow with fire
And the crowd aroused with hate.
Did you sleep well, old Vienna?
It was late.

They broke into the temples,
They broke into the stores.
So well behaved, good friends and neighbors
Double-locked their doors.
Oh, it's just the Jew.
What else is new?

Now, friends, I look around me—
I see nobody's learned.
Seems there's no way to feel the pain
Till it's your own face that's burned.
Too late to make amends,
My story ends.

# NE CSÜGGEDJ
## Do Not Despair

I first became aware of the nature of Nazi anti-Semitism in my early childhood when Jewish refugees from Germany arrived at our still-untouched Czechoslovakia, bringing the first accounts of the Nazi regime. One day, such a family of Jewish refugees, the Guttmans from Hamburg, showed up in Galanta, my hometown. They were German Jews of Eastern origin, and therefore among the first targets of Nazi harassment. Mr. Guttman had already been detained in Dachau, one of the original Nazi concentration camps. When he was released after a few months, the entire family fled Germany. The Guttmans were helped by the Jewish community in Galanta, of which my father was president. Improvised lodgings were provided, and food, until employment was found for Mr. Guttman. Mr. Guttman's firsthand account of his experiences in Dachau were spread through the community in a hushed manner. Most people in Galanta were psychologically unprepared to believe his account, and even less able to consider the possibility that something similar might happen to them.

Occasionally my mother talked at length with Mr. Guttman, but we children were not allowed to hear those conversations. I managed once to sneak into the room where they were talking, and hiding behind the living room sofa, I listened to Mr. Guttman tell my mother about Dachau. At one point he described his abuse there: Bent down, with his hands touching his feet, he had to repeat, "I am a cursed, damned Jew," while an SS man whipped him.

Cringing in my hiding place, I felt every lash of the whip on my own body, lived every second of Mr. Guttman's humiliating experience. I was then six or seven years old. At that time we still enjoyed the freedom of our social democratic republic of Czechoslovakia, which had been headed by the idealistic president Tomáš Masaryk, a humanist, a scholar, and a lover of freedom and democracy, who was universally revered. Soon after his death, in 1937, the mutilation of Europe began. First Austria was annexed by Germany in 1938, then Czechoslovakia was dissected. Bohemia and Moravia, the northwestern sections of Czechoslovakia, were made into a German protectorate, and autonomy was granted to the greater part of Slovakia, except for a strip of land along its southern border, which was awarded to Hungary in return for the cooperation of its government in Germany's war efforts. The Jews in our area had been extremely apprehensive at the prospect of becoming part of the newly independent Slovakia, which had a strongly fascistic government. Annexation to Hungary, though its government was also anti-Semitic, was the better of two evils at that time. So when in November 1938 the radio announced that Galanta fell into the section which had become Hungarian, everyone sighed with relief.

Though the so-called Jewish Laws were already in effect in Hungary, restricting Jews from study at universities, barring them from many trades, businesses, and the media, there were as yet no open acts of violence or deportations. Thus, despite the restrictions and hardships, Jewish life in Hungary continued, Jewish schools and cultural activities flourished. Hungary at that time was also the refugee center of European Jews. Well-organized Zionist and other youth groups engaged in daring rescue activities across the Hungarian borders, and secretly harbored thousands of Jewish refugees from Nazi-occupied Slovakia, Austria, Poland, and Germany.

Hungarian Jews, traditionally imbued with loyalty toward their country, nurtured the illusion that they could avoid the fate of the rest of European Jewry. But in 1944, one year before the end of the war, the Germans did occupy Hungary. Many hoped that the Nazis, who were losing the war on all fronts, would not expend the time and effort to liquidate the Hungarian Jews. Contacts with high SS officials were secretly established for the purpose of seeking a deal to buy the lives of Hungarian Jews. Adolf Eichmann, the commander of Jewish affairs in Hungary, proposed the release of about one million Jews then living in Hungary, including many refugees from other countries, in exchange for ten thousand trucks, eight hundred tons of coffee, two hundred tons each of cocoa and tea, a million bars of soap, and a large amount of sugar. This was, in Eichmann's words, a "goods for blood" deal. The person in charge of negotiating for the Jews was Joel Brand, who was allowed to travel to neutral Turkey to transmit Eichmann's offer to world Jewry and, through them, to the Allies. The Allies did not trust the offer and were not inclined to pay this ransom for the release of Jews.

With the help of the zealous Hungarian Nazis, the Nyilasok, the efficient, rapid, and merciless deportation of Hungarian Jews followed. Within two months after the collapse of negotiations—that is, by August 1944—all of Hungary's Jews, with the exception of those in Budapest, were deported, most of them to Auschwitz. Four hundred thousand Hungarian Jews were murdered in these last months of the war.

* * *

"Notice is hereby given that all Jews of Galanta must move to the quarters designated for them as ghetto within twenty-four hours," was the message the town crier announced on all street corners. My father came in from the street white as a ghost. He went into my grandmother's apartment, and I could hear their mournful lamentations. That evening, a kind of end-of-the-world atmosphere dominated all Jewish homes. Our housekeeper fainted, and the doctor had to be called. It was surprising that he was available, because many people became ill that night from shock and heartbreak.

Fortunately, my mother busied herself with baking up all the flour, sugar, and honey into cookies to be taken along to the ghetto. I was glad to help her; it comforted me.

When everyone had gone to sleep, I went out by myself to our porch. It was early in May, and the garden was already in bloom. I said goodbye to it. The night was black. Not a star, not a breeze: total silence. I stayed out for a long time, reluctant to give up these last peaceful moments. Then suddenly the darkness became hostile. Thousands of menacing figures seemed to lurk in the soundless treetops. Shadows, ghosts, hangmen's silhouettes, surrounded me. It was time to go into the house, into my own bed for the last time. Tomorrow we would be in the ghetto.

The next day the Hungarian Gestapo and gendarmes went from house to house to make sure that nothing valuable was taken along by the Jews. After this inspection, we had to leave our home carrying our bundles and walk to the ghetto, which was around the street where the synagogue was located.

"Ne csüggedj, ne sirjál bús Izrael" (Don't despair, do not weep, sad Israel) is a song closely connected to my memory of these times. My sister Judith, eleven years old then, brought it home from the improvised classroom in which the younger children spent the day. They were taught, among other things, encouraging songs like "Ne Csüggedj" to boost their spirits and to distract them from the oppressive atmosphere that prevailed everywhere. It is not known who put the song together; most likely it was a local teacher who did not survive. Judith sang it to us with great enthusiasm, which cheered us up.

Judith Kalisch, 1932–1944.

# NE CSÜGGEDJ
## Do Not Despair

(In Hungarian)
Author unknown

Ne csüg - gedj, ne sir - jál, bús Iz-ra-el. El-mul - nak a ne - héz ó - rák. Büsz - kén vi-seld el ezt az i-dőt, Nyil - nak még ker - ted-ben ró - zsák.

Don't de-spair don't weep, oh, sad Is-ra-el, Soon will end these sor - row-ful hours.___ Bear these dread-ful times with__ pride; Your gar-den yet will bloom with__ flow - ers. Your

Tá - ma-szod le - gyen az if - jú se - reg
strength will come from le - gions of young

Friss dal - lal mun - ká - ra
Read - y to work with fresh

ké - szen,
song.

Aj - kun-kon dal van szi - vünk-ben hit,
A song on our lips and faith in our hearts,

Ki
In

hisz a vi - har - ban sem vész el.
storms the be - liev - ers stay strong.

Zász - lón - kon jel - sza-vunk
Love is the watch-word

a sze - re-tet,
on our flag,

Hir - det jük mer - re csak já - runk.
We he-rald it wher-ev-er we may be.

Ne csüggedj, ne sirjál, bús Izrael.
Elmulnak a nehéz órák.
Büszkén viseld el ezt az időt
Nyilnak még kertedben rózsák.

Támaszod legyen az ifjú sereg
Friss dallal munkára készen.
Ajkunkon dal van szivünkben hit
Ki hisz a viharban sem vész el.

Zászlónkon jelszavunk a szeretet
Hirdetjük merre csak járunk.
Csak fel a fejjel előre nézz
Még győzni fog ez a nép!

*Don't despair, don't weep, oh, sad Israel.*
*Soon will end these sorrowful hours.*
*Bear these dreadful times with pride;*
*Your garden yet will bloom with flowers.*

*Your strength will come from legions of young*
*Ready to work with fresh song.*
*A song on our lips and faith in our hearts,*
*In storms the believers stay strong.*

*Love is the watchword on our flag,*
*We herald it wherever we may be.*
*Lift up your hearts and look straight ahead:*
*This people yet will be free!*

# NURSERY RHYME FOR DEAD CHILDREN

In 1975, Peter Wortsman, then twenty-three years old, accompanied a group of Holocaust survivors on a return visit to the former extermination camp of Auschwitz, which had been transformed into a state museum by the Polish government. Wortsman made this trip, as he had his first, two years before, on a Thomas J. Watson fellowship, to study and interview these survivors.

"Wild grass grows around the rusty rails on which the trains with human freight coasted to a final stop. It also grows through the cracked cement floor of the crematorium . . ." reads Peter Wortsman's description of the Auschwitz grounds. The visitors were shown stacks of suitcases, clothing, shoes, toys, dishes, and spoons—belongings taken from the victims before they were gassed. Piles of human hair and bones and other grim reminders of the extermination process were also on exhibit. "Nursery Rhyme for Dead Children" was Wortsman's response to what he saw.

Wortsman's lyrics speak of a hungry boy who never came back. Peter told me that he was moved to write the song after he happened to find a small spoon on the grounds of Auschwitz.

"Nursery Rhyme for Dead Children" brings to life the memory of my own deportation. The rhythm of the song recalls the rattle of the freight train in which, in June 1944, we were taken to Auschwitz. First our bundles were thrown into the cattle cars and the small children placed on top of the pile. Then seventy-five to a hundred people were pushed into each car and a few loaves of bread tossed in with them. Finally, two buckets, one filled with water and one left empty for excrement, were put into each wagon. Then the door was locked and barred from the outside. We traveled thus for three days and nights.

There was scarcely any air inside the cattle car. Two of the four tiny windows were boarded up, the other two covered with barbed wire, crisscrossed. Movement in the cramped wagon was practically impossible, but somehow I managed to climb over to where my mother was and stayed there, pressed against her body, during the harrowing three-day journey. The memory of her closeness in those last hours of her life has always stayed with me.

When we arrived in Auschwitz we were numb and dazed. We climbed off the cattle cars to the shrill commands of the SS. We did not yet know what the four black smoking chimneys in the landscape meant, nor did we know the significance of our forced division into two groups. Before our deportation, the Hungarian authorities had told us that we were going to be relocated, and that elderly people and small children would be taken care of, while the others would be sent to work.

The Nazis used this lie everywhere to avoid panic among the deportees. When I saw that mothers and small children were allowed to remain together, I assumed that they were to be treated more gently. Quickly I detached my little sister Judith, whose arms were intertwined with mine and those of my older sister, Nany, and I motioned her over to where my mother and grandmother stood. Later, we learned that the older people and little children had been taken straight to the gas chambers. Nothing could console me regarding this tragic episode, not even the fact that a few days later, children younger than thirteen, as was my sister, were removed from our barracks by the SS, never to be seen again.

Judith was a sunny child, the much-loved baby of the family. I remember that when we first walked to the ghetto, we clung to each other. Judith cried quietly and asked over and over, "Why? Why?" I tried to find an answer, but couldn't.

# NURSERY RHYME FOR
# DEAD CHILDREN

Words and Music by
PETER WORTSMAN

4. You'll find the spoon in a rust-y pile, Go dig it
5. You'll find the boy___ a-mong the bones. Go drag him

(2nd time)

up, go dig it up. You'll find the spoon in a rust-y pile. Go
out, go drag him out. You'll find the boy___ a-mong the bones. And

(2nd time)

try and dig it up.___
he will nev-er come back.___

*diminuendo*

*rallentando*

*ppp*

A spoon ran over the railroad track
And never came back, and never came back.
A spoon ran over the railroad track
And it did not come back.

A hungry boy he held the spoon
And never came back, and never came back.
A hungry boy he held the spoon
And he did not come back.

Where did you put my spoon and boy
That never came back, that never came back?
Where did you put my spoon and boy?
For they did not come back.

You'll find the spoon in a rusty pile—
Go dig it up, go dig it up!
You'll find the spoon in a rusty pile—
Go try and dig it up!

You'll find the boy among the bones—
Go drag him out, go drag him out!
You'll find the boy among the bones—
And he will never come back.

# TSEN BRIDER
## Ten Brothers

Since World War II, Auschwitz has been so universally identified as the largest center of Nazi genocide that it is difficult to visualize it as Oswiecim, the peaceful shtetl town of Orthodox Jews in Upper Silesia, Poland, the place it had been before the war. When the Germans occupied Poland, the Jews buried most of their sacred books, the *s'forim* and *gemores,* so that these should not be desecrated by the enemy. A number of their books and scrolls they packed into the bundles of belongings they were allowed to take along when they were herded toward deportation. It was a long way to the cattle wagons, and as the bundles became too heavy to carry, the former residents of Oswiecim had to drop most of their contents on the road. These were eagerly grabbed by a jeering anti-Semitic crowd trailing the Jews behind. They picked up everything of the dropped goods except for the sacred books, which lay strewn about, "littering" the streets of Oswiecim. This was in the spring of 1941.

In December of that same year, the initial barracks of the infamous death camp Auschwitz were erected by its first inmates, many of them Russian prisoners of war. Most of these inmates died of exposure during that winter.

The Auschwitz I knew was its Birkenau compound, where we stood for hours on roll calls, beginning at three o'clock in the morning. When the guards and "Kapos"—overseers—were not looking, my sister Nany, who stood behind me, would hug me from time to time, to warm and protect me from the cold winds that blew at dawn even in July and August. Then we changed roles and I hugged and protected her. Our eyes were always riveted on the sky to avoid looking at the scenery around us, and because up above us we were granted the rare spectacle of those unusual sunrises: vivid red and rosy sunrays bursting through delicate white clouds against the deep-blue Silesian sky. This heavenly phenomenon felt like a cruel joke, juxtaposed against the bleak desolation that surrounded us, the black smoke and the stench from the chimneys of the four crematoriums burning day and night in Birkenau, the Auschwitz I knew in 1944.

Amidst this landscape of smoke and barbed wire, populated by skeleton-like prisoners and death marchers, an orchestra played on an elevated platform and could be seen and heard over a considerable area. At certain times of the day the musicians were ordered by the SS to play merry tunes: for the arrival of new transports, the marching of prisoners to the gas chambers, public punishments, and executions on the gallows. To hear frivolous, lighthearted music as accompaniment to these events was an even more unspeakable mockery than the sight of the joyful sunrises in the skies over Auschwitz.

Alexander Kulisiewicz, 1918–1982.

On three occasions I was able to see the orchestra from very close up, twice when we were marched to *Entlausung*—shower and disinfection—and again when they took to the trains seventy-five of us who had been selected for transfer to a slave labor camp. The musicians' uniforms were white, with a single broad stripe of red painted down the center of the back. On their shaven heads they wore white sailor-type caps painted red across the center. Their faces chalk-white, their empty gazes unfocused, they played with stiff, abrupt motions, like ghost musicians of the "brave new hell" called Auschwitz. For years after the war, whenever I went to a concert, the orchestra in the hall fused with my memory of the Auschwitz musicians.

This haunting image is made vivid by the song "Tsen Brider." A very popular old Yiddish folk song similar to "Ten Little Indians," the original "Tsen Brider" told the story of ten brothers who, one after another, die of cold, hunger, or other suffering. It was sung and played by poor traveling Jewish musicians to elicit sympathy and a few pennies from their listeners in the streets.

Martin Rosenberg, a Polish-Jewish musician, wrote this version of "Tsen Brider" during his imprisonment in the concentration camp of Sachsenhausen. Rosenberg, known professionally before the war as Rosebery d'Arguto, had been the conductor of a workmen's chorus in Neuköln, a suburb of Berlin. He was arrested as a socialist and Jew in 1939 and sent to Sachsenhausen, where he was brutally tortured. As soon as he recovered, he organized and conducted a clandestine chorus of twenty-five Jewish prisoners, who would perform secretly in the less closely guarded barracks where political prisoners were held. When it became known that the Jewish prisoners of Sachsenhausen were to be transferred to Auschwitz, Rosenberg wrote this version of "Tsen Brider," in which the ten brothers are murdered, one after the other, in the gas chambers. Before the tenth brother must die, he wants to sing a last song and asks the musicians to accompany him. The song ends: "We hurt no one, we did no wrong."

Martin Rosenberg and his chorus were deported from Sachsenhausen to Auschwitz in 1942. They all died in the gas chambers in 1943.

I learned "Tsen Brider" and the story of its origins from Alexander Kulisiewicz, a Polish writer, musician, and singer who was detained as a non-Jewish political prisoner in Sachsenhausen for six years. He knew Rosebery d'Arguto and his chorus and was present at their last rehearsal before they were transferred to Auschwitz. D'Arguto asked Kulisiewicz not to forget "Tsen Brider," and if he should survive, to sing the song and through it tell the world of the suffering in the death camps. Kulisiewicz kept his promise. After the war he devoted his life to making the songs of the concentration camps known all over the world. He toured Europe, Japan, and the United States with his program of "Songs from the Depths of Hell." I met him on both his stays in New York. He was an ailing, frail man, who told me that only his mission to sing these songs kept him alive. He impressed me deeply with his determination. After his second visit here, in 1980, his health deteriorated rapidly. I decided to visit him in Krakow in December 1981. The trip had to be canceled because of the political unrest in Poland at that time. I hoped to see him as soon as traveling to Poland was possible again, but to my grief, he died just three months later, in March 1982. In his last letters he pleaded with me repeatedly to continue his work, to sing the songs of the concentration camps. I promised to do so as long as I live.

# TSEN BRIDER
## Ten Brothers

Music by Rosebery D'Arguto
After an old Yiddish folksong

**Faster**
*(Tempo II)*

Tsen bri - der ze - nen mir ge - ven,___ Hobn mir ge-
*Ten hap - py broth-ers were* *we to-geth-er,* *We lived by*

han-dlt mit vayn. Ey - ner iz ge - shtor - bn, Ze - nen mir ge-
*deal-ing in wine.* *One of us died ear - ly,* *And so we re-*

bli - bn nayn.___ Oy, oy, oy,___ oy.___
*mained___ nine.___ Oy, oy, oy,___ oy.___*

**Pesante**

Yi - dl mi - tn fi - dl,___ Moy-she mi - tn bas,
*Yi - dl with the fid - dle,___ Moy-she with the bass,*

Shpil-zhe mir a li – dl, Men firt undz in dem gas.___
*Play for us a lit – tle, The gas cham-ber we face.___*

Yi – dl mi – tn fi – dl, Moy – she mi – tn bas,
*Yi – dl with a fid – dle, Moy – she with the bass,*

Shpil-zhe mir a li – dl, men firt undz in dem gas.___
*Play for us a lit – tle, the gas cham-ber we face.___*

53

**Tempo I**

Bom bom bom bom bom bom bom bom bom bom bom bom

**Tempo II** *(Faster)*

bom bom.____ Eyn bru – der nor bin ikh ge –
One broth – er on – ly I re –

bli – bn, Mit vem'n zol ikh vey – nen?____ Di
main,____ With whom shall I____ sigh?____

an – de – re hot men der-har – get, Tsi ge-denkt ir zey – er
All____ the____ oth-ers cold – ly killed, Re – mem – ber them and

54

ney – men. Oy, oy, oy,_____ oy._____
cry._____ Oy, oy, oy,_____ oy._____

**Tempo III**

Yi – dl mi – tn fi – dl, Moy – she mi – tn bass,
Yi – dl with the fid – dle, Moy – she with the bass,

Hert mayn letst_ li – dl, men firt mikh oykh tsum gas._____
Let me sing my last_ song, the gas cham – ber I face._____

Yi – dl mi – tn fi – dl, Moy – she mi – tn bass,
Yi – dl with the fid – dle, Moy – she with the bass,

55

Hert mayn letst__ li - dl. Tsen bri-der__ ze-nen mir__ ge-
*Let me sing my last__ song.__ Ten hap-py__ broth-ers were__ we to-*

Tempo I

ven Mir ho-bn key-nem nit vey ge - ton. Li-lay, li -lay,
*geth-er We hurt__ no one, and did no wrong. Li-lay, li -lay,*

li - lay. Li-lay, li-lay, li - lay.__
*li - lay. Li-lay, li-lay, li - lay.__*

Tsen brider zenen mir geven;
Hobn mir gehandlt mit vayn.
Eyner iz geshtorbn—
Zenen mir geblibn nayn.
Oy, oy, oy, oy.

*Refrain*
*Yidl mitn fidl,*
Moyshe mitn bas,
Shpil-zhe mir a lidl,
Men firt undz in dem gas.

Eyn bruder nor bin ikh geblibn,
Mit vem zol ikh veynen?
Di andere hot men derharget—
Tsi gedenkt ir zeyer neymen.
Oy, oy, oy, oy.

*Refrain*
*Yidl mitn fidl,*
Moyshe mitn bas,
Hert mayn letst lidl
Men firt mikh oykh tsum gas.

Tsen brider zenen mir geven—
Mir hobn keynem nit vey geton.

Ten happy brothers were we together,
We lived by dealing in wine.
One of us died early—
And so we remained nine.
Oy, oy, oy, oy.

Refrain
*Yidl with the fiddle,*
*Moyshe with the bass,*
*Play for us a little,*
*The gas chamber we face.*

One brother only I remain.
With whom shall I sigh?
All the others coldly killed—
Remember them and cry.
Oy, oy, oy, oy.

Refrain
*Yidl with the fiddle,*
*Moyshe with the bass,*
*Let me sing my last song,*
*The gas chamber I face.*

Ten brothers were we together—
We hurt no one and did no wrong.

# VARSHE
## Warsaw

Warsaw, a glittering metropolis before World War II, became the site of a dreary, overcrowded ghetto of about 550,000 Jews after the German assault on Poland. A three-meter-high wall surrounded the ghetto, a confined area in which an average of thirteen people were crammed into each room. The food ration was 184 calories per person per day. Fifty percent of the ghetto population starved to death or died in epidemics, and thousands were deported to Treblinka and other death camps.

From April 19 to May 8, 1943, this ghetto was the scene of the most dramatic underground revolt of the war, in which the 50,000 Jews who had survived the starvation, torture, and deportations rose up against their Nazi tormentors and fought to the last bullet and the last man.

The first reports of the Warsaw ghetto uprising came on April 19, through messages sent over a clandestine radio station:

> The survivors of the Warsaw ghetto have begun an armed resistance against the murderers of the Jewish people. . . . The ghetto is aflame. . . . We shall attack the enemy with whatever weapons are available—with knives, axes, clubs, acid—to prevent further deportations to the death camps. . . . We shall not surrender; this is a struggle for our freedom, human dignity, and honor. . . . We shall avenge the crimes committed in Auschwitz, Treblinka, Belsen, Maidanek. . . . Through the flames and smoke of the burning ghetto and the blood of our brothers and sisters, we, the besieged in the Warsaw ghetto, send you brotherly greetings. . . . Long live freedom! . . . Long live liberty! . . .

The revolt was neither a sudden happening nor a simple reaction to the atmosphere of terror which had prevailed from the first day of the ghetto. It was carefully planned by a group of young people in their twenties who belonged to various youth organizations. Mordekhai Aniliewicz, affectionately called Aniolek—The Little Angel—by his friends, was made the leader of the revolt. A member of Hashomer Hatsair, a Zionistic youth movement which advocated communal, kibbutz life, Aniliewicz had founded an urban kibbutz in the ghetto long before the uprising. This kibbutz was the center for intense underground educational work. Its major task gradually became training and preparation for an armed revolt against the Germans. "We will not die in slow torment, but fighting," was their slogan. They began to organize the acquisition of ammunition—small arms, hand grenades, pistols, and dynamite. This was accomplished by a chain of people in and outside the ghetto.

In a letter dated March 13, 1943, Aniliewicz urgently requested arms from the Polish underground resistance movement and the Russian partisans, but very little assistance was forthcoming from them. There was no response from the Allied powers, either, although repeated personal messages reached London and the United States. Since the revolt of the Warsaw ghetto was deemed neither politically nor strategically important to any of the nations fighting the Germans, the ghetto fighters were forced to buy arms from the Poles at exorbitant cost and at insane risk of life. The arms had to be dismantled and smuggled into the ghetto piece by piece, through holes dug at night in the walls. All these efforts called for superhuman daring, patience, deftness, and determination.

While these preparations for the fighting were being made, the ghetto itself was readied. Inhabitants constructed hideouts in attics and cellars, subterranean shelters, and a maze of connecting corridors. The entire ghetto population prepared to move underground.

On April 19, two thousand SS troops, under the command of Major General Jürgen Stroop, entered the ghetto, while German, Ukrainian, and Lithuanian patrols surrounded it. The ghetto fighters threw incendiary bottles at the SS and one of the German tanks was burned out by the explosives. Shocked at the Jewish resistance, the Germans withdrew. The ghetto rejoiced: white-and-blue flags were hoisted, and although everyone knew that the Germans would return, people hugged, kissed, and laughed. The next day, one hundred Germans were killed by a land mine.

On April 21, heavily armed German units moved in and started bonfires. During the next few days, flamethrowers forced thousands of Jews out of their hiding places. Thousands more were burned alive in the shelters, yet the fighting went on. Desperate messages were broadcast, pleading for rifles, machine guns, explosives, but no help came.

Yitskhak Zuckerman, who lived in hiding outside the ghetto, was in charge of procuring weapons for the revolt. In his last letter to Zuckerman, Mordekhai Aniliewicz wrote: "I don't know if we'll see each other again. . . . I cannot describe to you the conditions under which we exist here. . . . In all the bunkers it is already impossible to light a candle for lack of air. . . . Our fate is sealed. . . . Keep well. . . . What's most important—the dream of my life—became reality. I lived to see Jewish defense in the ghetto in all its greatness."

Mordekhai Aniliewicz, 1918–1943.

The ghetto fighters held out for three weeks, and "every threshold in the ghetto became a fortress." The Germans used poison gas to "flush out" these fortresses. On May 8, the Germans surrounded the last bunker—the headquarters of the ghetto fighters—at 18 Mila Street. The ghetto fighters had decided not to fall into the Germans' hands alive, and one by one they killed each other. Aniliewicz, their beloved and legendary leader, wrapped himself in a white-and-blue flag, we are told, and jumped into the flames of the ghetto. Just ten of the ghetto fighters were able to escape, through the sewers. To bear witness to the uprising became their life's task.

To commemorate the first anniversary of the Warsaw ghetto uprising, the Vilna poet Shmerke Kaczerginski wrote the poem "Varshe." This was in the spring of 1944, during the last phase of the war, while Kaczerginski was in the forests of Narotsh (ninety kilometers from Vilna), fighting with his partisan unit. "Varshe" conveys to us the unforgettable events of the uprising and the ghetto fighters' determination to regain self-respect and dignity through resistance.

"Varshe" was set to music by the composer Leon Wainer. Born in Lodz in 1898, Wainer fled to Russia to escape the Germans at the beginning of the war and returned to Poland after the defeat of the Axis. There he met Kaczerginski, who inspired him to give the poem a musical setting.

# VARSHE
## Warsaw

Words by Shmerke Kaczerginski

Music by Leon Wainer

shvindt nit    di nakht    un der    tog    kumt    nit on,    A
*night    does-n't end    and the    lead-en    hours___ drag,    The*

blu-ti-ke koyl vert di erd shoyn.    A yid fla-tert oyf    vi a
*earth    is    like blood-y___ coals.___    The Jew___    a-ris-es like a*

shtur - mi - she fon, A fon i - nem tol fun di mey - sim. A
*storm - tossed flag,* *A flag in the val-ley of dead souls.* *A*

yid fla - tert oyf vi a shtur - mi - she fon, A fon i - nem tol fun di
*Jew a - ris - es like a storm - tossed flag, A flag in the val-ley of dead*

**1.** *etc.* | **Fine**

mey - sim. | mey - sim. Krits oys zikh in har - tsn dray
*souls.* | *souls.* *Three words etched in blood in our*

ver - ter fun blut: Ne - ko - me! Ne - ko - me! Ne - ko - me!
*hearts will re - main:* *Re - venge! Re - venge! Re - venge!*

62

S'farshvindt nit di nakht un der tog kumt nit on,
A blutike koyl vert di erd shoyn.
A yid flatert oyf vi a shturmishe fon,
A fon inem tol fun di meysim.

In khurves dos geto, di yidn in shlakht.
Der yid shprayzt durkh roykh un durkh flamen.
Nekome! Nekome! Es shturemt di nakht,
Far kinder, far tates, far mames!

Der shney shit un shit un di erd vert nit vays.
Es halt nokh dos blut in eyn zidn.
Es ruft nokh nekome oyf shneyikn ayz—
Dos blut fun di heldishe yidn.

Keyn tog vet nit zayn, ruft der yid, un keyn nakht.
Mir veln di velt nit fargebn!
Di velkhe zaynen gefaln in shlakht
Eybik in undz veln lebn!

Mir veln gedenken dem vey un dem mut,
Es fibert in gli di neshome.
Krits oys zikh in hartsn dray verter fun blut:
Nekome! Nekome! Nekome!

*The night does not end and the leaden hours drag,*
*The earth is like bloody coals.*
*The Jew arises like a storm-tossed flag,*
*A flag in the valley of dead souls.*

*The ghetto is in shambles—oh, the Jews all fight.*
*Through flame and smoke they stride.*
*Revenge! Revenge! They storm through the night,*
*For parents, for children, for pride!*

*The snow falls and falls, yet the earth is not white.*
*The red seething blood still shows through.*
*It calls for revenge on this icy night—*
*For the blood of the heroic Jew.*

*No day there will be, shouts the Jew, and no night.*
*The world we can never forgive!*
*Every man and woman who fell in the fight*
*In our hearts forever will live.*

*We shall always remember their courage and pain,*
*Our feverish souls will avenge.*
*Three words etched in blood in our hearts*
  *will remain:*
*Revenge! Revenge! Revenge!*

# ZOG NIT KEYN MOL
## Never Say

The early poetry of Hirsh Glick, like that of so many poets who die young, was full of premonition. At the age of eighteen, he wrote in "Amol" (Once Upon a Time): "I once dreamed I was the hero of a legend." That was in 1940, in the early stages of the war, when Vilna was not yet under German occupation.

Three years later, in April 1943, when the news of the Warsaw ghetto uprising reached the Vilna ghetto, Hirsh Glick wrote "Zog Nit Keyn Mol" (Never Say). Through this song he became not only a legend but a symbol of faith and spiritual defiance.

The song had an instant, immense impact and spread rapidly through the ghetto. People sang it in attics, in cellars, and in underground hideouts. They hummed its tune in the presence of German guards, during their slave labor work. The song spread from Vilna to other ghettos and then to concentration camps; it became a source of new hope and the hymn of the Jewish resistance fighters.

Who was this Hirsh Glick who, while still so young, captured in one song the essence of the Jewish resistance?

Hirsh, or Hirshke, as his friends called him, was born in Vilna into a working-class family. His father, an old-clothes dealer, was an exceedingly pious man, referred to frequently by others as a *lamed-vovnick,* one of the thirty-six "just men" for whose sake, according to Khassidic beliefs, the world is allowed to continue. His mother's family had many natural musicians, both singers and instrumentalists.

Hirshke began to write poetry at the age of thirteen, and at sixteen was cofounder of a talented group of young poets who called themselves Yungvald—Young Forest. He was a good-looking, popular boy and an excellent student. His first poems were written in Hebrew, but later he wrote in Yiddish. Because of his family's poverty, he had to end his studies prematurely, working for his living even as a youngster. He became an apprentice in a paper business and later worked in a hardware store.

When the Germans occupied Vilna in 1941, Hirshke was one of the thousands of young people who tried to join the partisans, but he was caught by the Germans and thrown into prison. After his release, he volunteered to go to Rzheshe, a camp built in a swamp about fourteen kilometers from Vilna. This unique "turf" camp accepted recruits who came voluntarily in the hope of treatment less harsh than they would receive in other camps. Hirshke became ill with typhoid fever and almost died. When the Rzheshe camp was dissolved, Hirshke was returned to the ghetto, where he participated in underground preparations for a revolt. He was also active in the literary-artistic circle of the Vilna ghetto, the group to which Zelig Kalmanowicz, Abraham

Hirsh Glick, 1920–1944.

Sutskever, Gershon Gladstein, Lea Rudnitsky, and many other notable poets and writers belonged. His poetry was acclaimed by this forum several times.

In 1943, when the Vilna ghetto was liquidated, Hirsh Glick was deported to Estonia. He was taken from one concentration camp to another—Nara, Kiviali, Azari, and finally Goldpilz. All had conditions so appalling that most of the inmates died. Hirsh survived until 1944, when the Russians were very close to Goldpilz. In July, he escaped into the forest and tried to join the partisan fighters. He was never heard of again. The Germans were combing the woods there, and it is presumed that Hirsh Glick was among those caught and executed.

Hirsh Glick wrote a great number of poems and songs, only a few of which survived through friends who hid them. His early work had become part of the archives at the Vilna ghetto, which were later found buried underground. He wrote in the ghetto, in the turf camp, and even in the worst of concentration camps in Estonia. Late at night, after a long day's grueling work, by the light of a kerosene lamp or a candle, on top of his wretched bunk, he wrote. When there was no pencil or paper, he recited his poems to his campmates, who memorized them. Many of his poems were written to well-known Jewish tunes of Russia and Poland. Such is the case of "Zog Nit Keyn Mol," which is set to a Russian melody.

Moyshe Gorin, who was with Hirshke in Rzheshe, tells how, while cutting and carrying heavy loads of turf ordinarily carried by horses, Hirsh would find a dry place in the swamp, sit down for a minute, and ask Gorin to hum a nice tune so that he could improvise words to it. In an early poem, "Fri-Friling" (Early Spring), he expresses outrage at any form of oppression:

> Why do I carry in me the rage of an arsonist,
> Why is my throat full of screams?

The powerful "Balade fun Broynem Teater" (Ballad of the Brown Theater) refers to the Nazis' brown shirts and tells of Vilna's Lukiszki prison, where many Jews spent days of horror and torture before their deaths.

Hirsh Glick's poems—even those composed in concentration camps—express belief in ultimate freedom. The last words of his "Turf Song," written in the Rzheshe swamp camp, are:

| | |
|---|---|
| *In dem bodn in dem kalten* | In the cold ground |
| *Ligt an oytser farbahaltn—* | Lies a precious stone hidden— |
| *Der bagin . . .* | The beginning . . . |

Glick's "Zog Nit Keyn Mol" served as the "precious stone" of a new beginning, an inspiration to the surviving postwar generation. Youth movements embraced it for its uplifting content. To the rhythm of "Zog Nit Keyn Mol," the first fighters for Israeli independence marched. It remains a universal song of courage.

# ZOG NIT KEYN MOL
## Never Say

Hirsh Glick

Marching tempo (♩ = 112)

Zog nit keyn mol az du geyst dem lets-tn veg, Khotsh him-len
*Nev-er say you've come to the end___ of the way,* *Though lead-en*

blay - e - ne far-shte-ln blo-ye teg. Ku-men vet nokh un-dzer oys-ge-benk-te
*skies blot out the light___ of the day.* *The hour___ we all long for will sure-ly ap-*

sho,
_pear,_

S'vet a poyk ton un – dzer trot: "Mir zay – nen
_Our steps will thun – der with the words:__"We are_

do! "
_here! "_

Ku – men vet nokh un – dzer oys – ge – benk – te
_The hour __ we all long for will sure – ly ap-_

sho,
_pear,_

S'vet a poyk ton un – dzer trot: "Mir zay – nen
_Our steps will thun – der with the words:__"We are_

1. _Etc._

do! "
_here! "_

8vg-----

Fine

do! "
here! "

Zog nit keyn mol az du geyst dem letstn veg,
Khotsh himlen blayene farshteln bloye teg.
Kumen vet nokh undzer oysgebenkte sho—
S'vet a poyk ton undzer trot: Mir zaynen do!

Fun grinem palmenland biz vaytn land fun shney,
Mir kumen on mit undzer payn, mit undzer vey;
Un vu gefaln iz a shprits fun undzer blut,
Shprotsn vet dort undzer gvure, undzer mut.

S'vet di morgnzun bagildn undz dem haynt,
Un der nekhtn vet farshvindn mitn faynt.
Nor oyb farzamen vet di zun un dem kayor—
Vi a parol zol geyn dos lid fun dor tsu dor.

Dos lid geshribn iz mit blut un nit mit blay,
S'iz nit keyn lidl fun a foygl oyf der fray.
Dos hot a folk tsvishn falndike vent—
Dos lid gezungen mit naganes in di hent!

Never say you've come to the end of the way,
Though leaden skies blot out the light of the day.
The hour we all long for will surely appear—
Our steps will thunder with the words: We are here!

From lands of palm trees to far-off lands of snow,
We come with anguish, we come with grief,
  with pain and woe;
And where our blood flowed right before our eyes,
There our power'll bloom, our courage will arise.

The glow of morning sun will gild a bright today,
Night's darkness vanish, like the enemy cast away.
But if we perish before this dawn's begun—
This song's a message passed to daughter and to son.

In blood this song was written, and not with pen
  or quill,
Not from a songbird freely flying as he will.
Sung by a people crushed by falling walls—
Sung with guns in hand, by those whom
  freedom calls!

69

# SHTIL, DI NAKHT IZ OYSGESHTERNT
## The Quiet Night Is Full of Stars

"Shtil, Di Nakht Iz Oysgeshternt," also known as "Partisanerlid," recounts the heroic deeds of a female resistance fighter. The young woman who inspired Hirsh Glick to write this song was Vitke Kempner, who, in 1942, participated in the first successful diversionary sabotage act of the Jewish partisans of Vilna. Vitke and fellow partisan Itzik Matzkevitch were instrumental in blowing up a train that carried two hundred German soldiers. It was she who, in the dark of night, surveyed the cold, muddy woods along the railroad tracks to determine the best spot to place the homemade explosives her unit had prepared. After this successful mission, she was made the leader of a reconnaissance group, and many important tasks were carried out under her daring direction. She once succeeded in smuggling herself into Kailis, a concentration camp near Vilna, and led a large group of its inmates safely into the forests. Captured and about to be turned over to the Gestapo, she eluded her guards by sheer cunning and dexterity, risking death by gunfire rather than submit to Gestapo torture.

But it would be unfair to praise only one of the countless courageous Jewish women of World War II, without whose help the rescue and resistance work of the underground movement would not have been possible. Most of these heroines were very young at the time, born at the end of or right after World War I, án era when girls had certainly not been raised to handle guns, to blow up bridges, or to carry on espionage or sabotage. This is implied in the second verse of "Shtil, Di Nakht," in which Glick admires the "girl with velvet face" who held up the enemy's caravan.

These young women did far more than hold up caravans during the Nazi occupation. They were the nerve centers of the resistance movement. They were messengers, they carried food, documents, and medical supplies, smuggled weapons into the ghettos and forests. Theirs was the job of maintaining the links between Jews in different ghettos, and between the ghettos and the outside world. It was they who brought news of the massacres of the Vilna and Kovno ghettos to the inhabitants of the then still relatively quiet ghettos of Warsaw, Bialystok, Grodno, and others, urging and helping them to organize resistance.

In order to perform these functions, some women assumed false Aryan identities, using forged documents. (Women could conceal their Jewishness much more easily than men, for no matter how "un-Jewish" a man looked, when caught by the Nazis he could easily be identified as Jewish by his circumcision, a practice virtually unknown among non-Jews at that time in Europe.)

Not only did they need an "Aryan" look—preferably blond hair and blue eyes;

they also had to speak Polish fluently and without a trace of Jewish accent or intonation. With their false identification papers, they were able to operate freely outside the ghetto as long as they were not found out or betrayed. Thus they saved thousands by smuggling food into the ghetto.

Many individual acts of great daring and courage have gone unrecorded, but some of these women have become legendary.

Sonia Madeisker was among the founders of the Vilna underground movement. She lived as an Aryan in the city, and tirelessly carried messages, food, and guns to and from the partisans. She helped Jews trapped in their bunkers under the ruins of the liquidated ghetto to escape to the forests. Only a few months before Vilna was liberated, she was caught by Gestapo soldiers. As they approached her, she shot seven of them. With the last bullet she tried to kill herself, but was only wounded. The Gestapo healed her wounds so that they could try to extract information from her about the partisans' whereabouts. They broke all her limbs, but she told them nothing. She was tortured to death.

Leonie Kazibrodski was a language teacher before the war. A woman of unusual beauty, she was a daredevil. She bought arms wherever she could get them, from Poles and even from Germans, delivering them to the partisans. Tales are told how, while flirting with German soldiers, she made them unwittingly help her carry valises packed with the matériel and weapons she smuggled from place to place. She was arrested at Malkynia (near Treblinka) while on a mission, and was put into the dreaded Pawiak prison in Warsaw. From there she was sent to Auschwitz, where she died in March 1943.

Frumka Plotnicka traveled across Poland to bring news and encouragement to the remaining ghettos, and to help them organize for resistance. She was offered papers and a passport to escape to a neutral country, but did not want to leave her partisan friends. Sent to Bedzin to organize an uprising in the ghetto, she became the leader of the revolt and died fighting in a bunker there in August 1943.

Zofia Yamaika, a girl from a prominent Khassidic family, joined a partisan group while still in the Warsaw ghetto. She was arrested many times during her countless rescue missions, and barely managed to escape each time. In February 1943, the reconnaissance partisan unit to which she belonged was attacked by a large German

Sonia Madeisker, 1913–1944.

force. Zofia opened fire on the Germans with her machine gun, thus assuring the escape of most of her fellow partisans. She, however, was killed.

Rosa Robota, the heroine of the Auschwitz underground, helped to blow up one of the four crematoriums of Birkenau in October 1944. Niuta Teitelbaum, known as "Wanda" in her underground years, and one of its most fearless fighters, was highest on the Nazis' list of most wanted partisans. The list is long—Tsivia Lubetkin of the Warsaw ghetto; the couriers Zelda Treger, Tamara Schneiderman, Tosia Altman, Sara and Reizel Silber, and many others. Many of these women died martyrs' deaths; none of them, even under the most bestial torture, betrayed their friends or their cause.

"Shtil, Di Nakht Iz Oysgeshternt" is a tribute to these women, who in normal times would have sought life-affirming roles rather than becoming heroines of warfare.

When Khaika Grossman, a survivor of the Bialystok ghetto, was asked where all these women got their calm, their patience and fearlessness, she answered: "It was the calmness which our comrades felt before and during the battle. The battle was our watchword; this was the moment for which we waited and hoped."

"You see, you don't understand . . . you who were not there will never understand," said another of the surviving women fighters to Marie Syrkin, the author of *Blessed Is the Match*. "The best perished . . . you will never know how wonderful they were."

# SHTIL, DI NAKHT IZ OYSGESHTERNT

## IZ OYSGESHTERNT

### The Quiet Night Is Full of Stars

Hirsh Glick

Andante (♩=ca. 66)

Shtil, di nakht iz oys - ge - shte - rnt,
*Qui - et night so full of stars,*

Un - der frost hot shtark ge - brent. Tsi ge -
*Bit - ter frost bites at your hand. Do*

denk - stu vi ikh hob dikh ge - le - rnt,
*you_____ re - mem - ber when I showed you__ how To*

Hal - tn a shpay - er in di hent. Tsi ge -
*hold_____ a gun__ like a man. Do*

denk - stu vi ikh hob dikh ge - le - rnt,
*you_____ re - mem - ber when I showed you__ how To*

Hal - tn a shpay - er in di hent.
*hold_____ a gun__ like a man.*

Shtil, di nakht iz oysgeshternt,
Un der frost hot shtark gebrent.
Tsi gedenkstu vi ikh hob dikh gelernt
Haltn a shpayer in di hent.

A moyd, a peltsl un a beret,
Un halt in hant fest a nagan.
A moyd mit a sametenem ponim
Hit op dem soynes karavan.

Getsilt, geshosn un getrofn
Hot ir kleyninker pistoyl.
An oyto, a fulinkn mit vofn
Farhaltn hot zi mit eyn koyl.

Far tog, fun vald aroysgekrokhn,
Mit shney-girlandn oyf di hor.
Gemutikt fun kleyninkn nitsokhn
Far undzer nayem, frayen dor.

*Quiet night so full of stars,*
*Bitter frost bites at your hand.*
*Do you remember when I showed you how*
*To hold a gun like a man.*

*A girl in sheepskin and felt beret,*
*In her hand she held a gun so tight.*
*A girl with velvet face fresh as the day*
*Kept back the enemy's trucks all night.*

*She aimed at the target, shot and hit!*
*Her little gun seemed never to tire.*
*An enemy truck loaded with weapons*
*Was held by her unceasing fire.*

*At dawn she crawled from the woods,*
*Garlands of snow on her hair.*
*Her brave spirit gives all courage*
*To fight for our freedom everywhere.*

# ZIAMELE

The author of "Ziamele" is not known, and I was not able to find out in which ghetto the song was first sung. But much is known about the fate of the thousands of Ziameles who existed and suffered in the ghettos.

*Ziamele* is the Yiddish word for "little seed." A term of endearment, this name was given to a ghetto orphan whose real name was unknown. A little seed, a small human being, existing in the ghetto, nobody knows how—as did so many homeless children whose parents were killed by the Germans. They mingled with the ghetto population; their emaciated, shadowlike little bodies clothed in rags were a familiar sight on the ghetto streets. They slept in house entrances, stairwells—any shelter they could find. "Their cries and moans throughout the night were among the most unbearable experiences of ghetto life," wrote Dr. Emanuel Ringelblum in his Warsaw ghetto diary.

The problem of caring for the orphaned children in the ghettos was immense. At first, boarding homes were established for them, but with the increased roundups and massacres, the number of these orphaned children multiplied too rapidly for housing to be provided for all. Some of them attended the illegal ghetto schools (the Germans did not allow education in the ghetto), but the homeless usually dropped out after a few days, forced by the hunger that plagued them to take to the streets to find food. The older of these waifs were used by the Jewish authorities of the ghetto—the Judenrat—to transport food in handcarts from the supply stores to distribution centers and public soup kitchens. For this service, they were given food and clothing. Others organized into gangs, stole food from homes and from the supply rooms of the Judenrat. The younger ones just hung around wherever something to eat might be found, often tearing food from adults' hands and quickly digging their teeth into it before they could be forced to give it back.

Among the Ziameles of the ghettos there were real larger-than-lifesize heroes. In a small ghetto near Vilna, a little boy by the name of Moyshele became well known for his skill in sneaking out of the ghetto, finding food, and bringing it back to children even younger than himself. Hiding in an attic, he rescued and cared for five other children, six and seven years old, somehow finding enough food to keep them all alive. He even managed to save these little ones when the Germans staged one of their special roundups of children. At such times, the Nazis would send the grownups out for the whole day on a work assignment. In their absence, soldiers moved in with their attack dogs and collected the children, without having to deal with the cries of the parents. As often as not, they included the old and sick in their roundups and took them all to the place of their execution. It is from this fate that Moyshele kept himself and the children under his supervision for a remarkably long period of time.

Another heroic boy, who looked much older than his eleven years, volunteered to replace his frail father on a work assignment in German-occupied Deblin. He was taken to the Chenstokhov concentration camp, where he worked with the grownups under brutal conditions until the Germans discovered that he was just a child. They decided to hang him, but by a fluke he escaped. In their rage, the Germans beat, tortured, and hanged another, still younger child, who was even less capable of heavy manual labor.

Most adult ghetto dwellers were so oppressed just trying to escape the inferno that they could give scant attention to the abandoned children. There were exceptions, ordinary but compassionate people who helped with food and shelter whenever they could. Some leaders and teachers refused to abandon the orphans, and accompanied them even to death, often when they might otherwise have saved themselves. Some of these heroes, like Dr. Janusz Korczak, who remained with the children of his orphanage on their death march, are known to us. He stood by the children in his charge and died with them.

The first time I heard "Ziamele" was in a performance in New York City by the singer and folklorist Ruth Rubin. The song is included in her book *Jewish Folk Songs.*

# ZIAMELE

Author Unknown

Yeder ruft mikh Ziamele—
Oy, vi mir iz shver.
Kh'hob gehat a mamele—
Kh'hob zi shoyn nit mer.
Kh'hob gehat a tatele,
Hot er mikh gehit.
Itst bin ikh a shmatele,
Vayl ikh bin a yid.

*People call me Ziamele—*
*Little seed, they say.*
*Once I had a mamele—*
*They took her far away.*
*Once I had a tatele—*
*He dearly loved me too.*
*Now I'm like a little rag,*
*Because I am a Jew.*

Kh'hob gehat a shvesterl,
Iz zi mer nito—
Akh, vu bistu, Esterl,
In der shverer sho?
Ergets bay a beymele,
Ergets bay a ployt,
Ligt mayn bruder Shloymele,
Fun a daytsh getoyt.

Kh'hob gehat a heymele;
Itster iz mir shlekht.
Kh'bin vi a baheymele,
Vos der talyen shekht.
Got, kuk fun himele,
Oyf der erd arop.
Zi dokh vi dayn blimele
Rayst der gazlen op.

*Once I had a sister dear,*
*But now she too is gone—*
*Ah, where are you, Esterl,*
*I'm so all alone.*
*Underneath some distant tree,*
*Near a fence of wood,*
*Lies my brother Shloymele,*
*By a Nazi killed.*

*Once I had a cozy home;*
*Now nothing shelters me.*
*I'm like a luckless sheep,*
*Slaughtered senselessly.*
*God, look down from heaven,*
*On this earth you've made.*
*See your little flowers*
*Cut by a cruel spade.*

# RIFKELE DI SHABESDIKE
## Rifkele, the Sabbath Widow

Before the full horror of life under the Nazis had permeated the ghettos, young people used to seek the few secluded areas to meet, to romance, and to fall in love. They sang the fashionable tangos of the era, music popular for its passionate rhythms and melancholy tunes, which were so oddly suited to the ghetto mood. Often, new words were written to these melodies, creating the first ghetto love songs.

Circumstances in the ghettos soon became so oppressive that normal feelings of love between men and women were overshadowed by the daily struggle just to keep alive. The periodic roundups, daily arrests, beatings and torture, starvation, and the presence of emaciated children dampened sensual feelings. Still, a few original love songs were created here and there, and "Rifkele di Shabesdike," from the Bialystok ghetto, is one of them. Imbued with sadness, the song is a tender expression of a woman's longing for her beloved husband, who had been taken away from her, and of her fear for his fate.

The day after the Germans marched into Bialystok, a city in northeast Poland, in June 1941, the SS regiment under the notorious commandant Gustav Friedl drove Jewish families into the synagogue, which they then set on fire. About one thousand Jews burned to death. In a subsequent roundup, three hundred Jews chosen from the intelligentsia of the community were hunted down, beaten, loaded onto trucks, and taken away. This occurred on Thursday, July 3, 1941. The following Saturday, July 5, three thousand more Jewish men were taken by trucks to an unknown destination. Commandant Friedl told the Jews that for five kilograms of gold, two million Soviet rubles, silver, and other valuables, the men would be returned to the ghetto. The wives and mothers of the abducted men feverishly organized the collection of the ransom. Everybody responded generously: women gave all their jewelry, the wealthy gave large sums of money. When the ghetto emissaries delivered the money and valuables to the Gestapo, they were told that the men had been sent to labor and concentration camps and would not return. The emissaries reported this to the Judenrat, who decided to withhold the devastating news in order not to destroy hope in the ghetto for the men's return.

In reality, none of these men was alive at this point; they had all been shot at nearby Pietrasze immediately after being taken from the ghetto. They came to be called the Thursday and Saturday victims, their wives and mothers the Thursday and Saturday widows.

"Rifkele di Shabesdike" is about a Saturday widow who still hoped for the release

Peysakh Kaplan, 1870–1943.

of her husband. This sad love song, written by Peysakh Kaplan, achieved immediate popularity in the ghetto.

Peysakh Kaplan was a Jewish writer and social activist in Bialystok before the war. He had written with great love about his native city, calling it "the princess of towns." Bialystok was an important center of commerce and industry, as well as of religious and social life, for the 60,000 Jews who lived there before the war. (Another 350,000 Jews inhabited its environs.) It was the cradle of such important early Zionist movements as Hoveve Zion—Lovers of Zion—among whose prominent members was Dr. Ludwig Lazar Zamenhof, the creator of the international language Esperanto.

Peysakh Kaplan was also the chronicler of the ghetto. His diary was found after the war in the ghetto ruins. From it and other accounts we learn that after the initial roundups, the first year of the Bialystok ghetto was relatively quiet, for the Germans were exploiting the ghetto factories and workshops for production of supplies for their army. Ephraim Barash, the head of the Judenrat, hoped that through the economic profit derived from their work for the German war effort, the ghetto population might be saved. However, no efforts deterred the Nazis from their original plans, and between February 5 and 12, 1943, ten thousand Jews were taken from Bialystok to Treblinka and Maidanek for extermination. Those too weak from starvation to walk—and there were hundreds of them—were killed on the spot.

Shortly after these murders and deportations, Mordekhai Tennenbaum and Khaika Grossman were sent by the Warsaw ghetto fighters to organize an uprising in the Bialystok ghetto. "Don't allow yourselves to be destroyed; die with honor!" was the battle cry. Arms were purchased from Poles and stolen from German armories. Because the Bialystok ghetto had only a wooden fence around it (the Warsaw ghetto was surrounded by a solid wall), defense was very hard to establish.

There was no escape from the besieged ghetto. The battle, which began on August 6, 1943, lasted four days. Axes and crowbars were among the weapons used. The ghetto inmates fought to the last bullet and most of them died in battle. The ghetto was burned to the ground and the few survivors, including Barash, the Judenrat head, were sent to Maidanek.

During the last year of the ghetto's existence, Peysakh Kaplan lived in hiding under cramped conditions. From this place of concealment he witnessed but escaped the February slaughters and deportations. "People moved about like shadows, physically and mentally shattered, their gazes reflecting hopes extinguished, moving around automatically like lunatics," he wrote in his diary.

Unable to endure the physical stress, Kaplan became ill and died in March 1943. He was deeply mourned by the remaining ghetto population. Among the last entries in his diary we read: "We go to our death. Avenge us!"

"Rifkele," Kaplan's love song, has been left to us, however, as a reminder that tenderness and compassion existed even in those times.

# RIFKELE DI SHABESDIKE
## Rifkele, the Sabbath Widow

Peysakh Kaplan

Moderate Waltz tempo

*mp*

Riv - ke - le___ di___ sha - bes - di - ke; Ar - bet in fa -
*Riv - ke - le___ the___ Sab - bath wi - dow; Spins at the fac - t'ry*

brik. Dreyt a fo - dem tsu a fo - dem, Flekht tsu-noyf a
*wheel. Twists a thread a-round a thread,___ Turns rope a-round a*

shtrik.    Oy, di ge — to fints — te — re, Doy — ert a — zoy
reel.      Oh, the dark — ness of the ghet — to Lasts too long to

lang, _____ Un dos harts a — zoy far — klemt___
bear, _____ And the long — ing in her heart___

Tut ir a — zoy bang.
Breeds its sor — row there.

Rifkele di shabesdike
Arbet in fabrik;
Dreyt a fodem tsu a fodem,
Flekht tsunoyf a shtrik.
Oy, di geto fintstere,
Doyert azoy lang,
Un dos harts azoy farklemt
Tut ir azoy bang.

*Rifkele, the Sabbath widow*
*Spins at the fact'ry wheel;*
*Twists a thread around a thread,*
*Turns rope around a reel.*
*Oh, the darkness of the ghetto*
*Lasts too long to bear,*
*And the longing in her heart*
*Breeds its sorrow there.*

Ir getrayer Hershele
Iz avek, nito,
Zint fun yenem shabes on,
Zint fun yener sho.
Iz fartroyert Rifkele,
Yomert tog un nakht,
Un atsind baym redele
Zitst zi un zi trakht.

Vu iz er, mayn libinker—
Lebt er nokh khotsh vu?
Tsi in kontsentratsye-lager
Arbet shver on ru?
Oy, vi finster iz im dort,
Biter iz mir do—
Zint fun yenem shabes on,
Zint fun yener sho.

*Her beloved Hershele*
*Is gone, is no more here,*
*Since that dreadful Saturday,*
*That hour so filled with fear.*
*Rifkele mourns her beloved,*
*Cries all night and day,*
*Spins at her spinning wheel*
*And broods the hours away.*

*Where is my beloved Hershele—*
*Does he still live somewhere?*
*In a concentration camp—*
*Have they sent him there?*
*Dark it is there for him,*
*Bitter for me here—*
*Since that dreadful Sabbath,*
*That hour so filled with fear.*

# TSIGAYNERLID
## Gypsy Song

In September 1941, a transport of one thousand Gypsies arrived at Lodz, in the second-largest ghetto in German-occupied Poland. Although Gypsies are Indo-Europeans and hence Aryan, they were persecuted and deported by the Nazis as "subhuman, asocial elements and saboteurs."

Forcing the Lodz Jews to vacate a small section of their ghetto, the Germans created a fenced-off compound for the Gypsies, who had been deported from Austria. Most of the Jews, wrapped in the daily tragedies of ghetto life, their energies sapped by starvation and squalor, paid little heed to the presence and fate of these Gypsies. Strictly quarantined and isolated from the rest of the ghetto, the Gypsies were easily ignored or forgotten. Thus it is all the more touching to hear a song describing the Gypsies' plight by the Lodz ghetto musician David Beigelman.

The Gypsies did not last long. Left without food for days, they were tortured sadistically by their special guards, who often forced them to do gymnastics until they

David Beigelman, 1877–1942.

collapsed or died. When, a few months later, a transport of three thousand more Gypsies was added to the crammed compound, a typhoid epidemic broke out. There were no health facilities. Doctors and nurses from the Jewish sector treated the sick, many of them dying with their patients. When the epidemic spread, hundreds of the afflicted were shot every day. The Nazi commander ordered squads of Jews to bury the Gypsies in the Jewish cemetery. Surviving Gypsies were deported to Auschwitz.

David Beigelman's "Tsigaynerlid" relates the attempts of these bewildered people to drown their suffering in song and dance. Beigelman had been a popular figure in Lodz's Jewish cultural life before the war. Born in 1887, he grew up in a family of nine siblings, each of whom played several instruments. A violinist, conductor, composer, and theater critic, Beigelman toured throughout Europe, and even visited the United States as a member of a theater orchestra.

During the Nazi occupation, Beigelman became the soul of the Lodz ghetto's cultural activities. He is remembered by survivors as one who remained optimistic and cheerful during the Nazi period, fighting demoralization, pessimism, and depression. He wrote many songs in the ghetto, expressing the tragedies of daily life there. Since Khaim Rumkowski, the chairman of the ghetto, had forbidden the singing of sad songs, most of Beigelman's works could be sung only in secret. Nevertheless, they became very popular, especially "Makh Tsu di Eygelekh" (Close Your Eyes), a lullaby, and "Nisht Keyn Rozhinkes mit Mandlen" (No Raisins and No Almonds), based on perhaps the best-known Yiddish song, "Rozhinkes mit Mandlen" (Raisins with Almonds). The Beigelman version describes the ordeal of death by starvation.

After the liquidation of the ghetto in May 1944, Beigelman was deported to Auschwitz. From there he was sent to a slave labor camp, where he died of exhaustion in February 1945, just three months before the liberation.

* * *

The area surrounding my hometown in Czechoslovakia was celebrated for its Gypsy musicians. I grew up hearing the melancholy or fiery, lilting melodies played by excellent Gypsy bands, not only at weddings and on holidays, but throughout the year. Gypsy musicians would wander from house to house, serenading villagers even in the middle of the night. I listened to them with endless, loving fascination.

When we were deported to Auschwitz, my sister and I were assigned to a barracks of "C" Compound at Birkenau, adjacent to the camp in which the Gypsies were detained. One thousand girls were housed in a barracks. We had to sleep draped around each other in fetal position; that was the only way we could fit in the space.

One night in early August, we heard spine-chilling shrieks coming from the Gypsy camp, augmented by the sound of trucks coming and going and the ferocious barking of dogs. The elder in charge of our barracks told us that the Gypsies were being taken away. The sound of the trucks, the barking of the dogs, and the screaming and wailing of the Gypsies permeated our camp throughout the night.

We held on to our shoes, our only possession aside from the single garment on our bodies, ready to run—which would of course have been useless—expecting in silent terror to be the next ones taken away. Feeling only my sister's and my heartbeats, I made up my mind not to scream when they came for us. The Gypsies, I thought, had been screaming for me too.

Three thousand Gypsies were taken to the gas chambers that August night in Auschwitz. In all, 500,000 Gypsies were killed by the Germans during World War II.

# TSIGAYNERLID
## Gypsy Song

Words and Tune by
David Beigelman

Fin-ster di nakht, vi koy-ln shvarts, Nor trakht un trakht, un s'klapt mayn harts. Mir tsi-gay-ner le-bn vi key-ner! Mir lay-dn noyt, ge-nug koym oyf broyt.

*Dark is the night, like black-est coal. I brood and brood, my heart-beats toll. We gyp-sies live like no oth-ers do.___ Suf-fer-ing pain,___ and hun-ger too.*

Dzum, dzum, dzum, dzum,_____ dzum, dzum,        Mir fli – en a-
*Dzum, dzum, dzum, dzum,_____ dzum, dzum,*        *Like sea gulls we*

rum vi di tshay – kes.        Dzum, dzum,___ dzum, dzum,___
*fly near and far.___*        *Dzum, dzum,___ dzum, dzum,___*

dzum, dzum,        Mir shpi – ln oyf di ba – la – lay – kes.
*dzum, dzum,*        *We're strum-ming our gyp – sy gui – tars._____*

**1.**

**2.**    Slow    D.S. 𝄉    Fine

lay – – kes.        lay – kes.___
*tars.___*        *tars.___*

D.S. 𝄉

90

Finster di nakht, vi koyln shvarts.
Nor trakht un trakht, un s'klapt mayn harts.
Mir tsigayner lebn vi keyner,
Mir laydn noyt, genug koym oyf broyt.

*Refrain*
Dzum, dzum, dzum...
Mir flien arum vi di tshaykes.
Dzum, dzum, dzum...
Mir shpiln oyf di balalaykes.

Nit vu men togt, nit vu men nakht;
A yeder zikh plogt, nor kh'trakht un trakht.
Mir tsigayner lebn vi keyner,
Mir laydn noyt, genug koym oyf broyt.

*(Refrain)*

---

*Dark is the night, like blackest coal.*
*I brood and brood, my heartbeats toll.*
*We Gypsies live like no others do,*
*Suffering pain, and hunger too.*

Refrain
*Dzum, dzum, dzum...*
*Like seagulls we fly near and far.*
*Dzum, dzum, dzum...*
*We're strumming our Gypsy guitar.*

*Nowhere to stay, almost no food;*
*Everyone struggles, but I just brood.*
*We Gypsies live like no others do,*
*Suffering pain, and hunger too.*

(Refrain)

# MOORSOLDATEN
## Peat Bog Soldiers

My first recollections of "Moorsoldaten" go back to my childhood, when it was erroneously considered to be a song from the Spanish Civil War. The reason for this confusion was probably that it had been made popular by Ernst Busch, a well-known German performer who fought in the International Brigade in Spain.

The birthplace of "Moorsoldaten," however, was Börgermoor, near Hanover, a concentration camp for political prisoners that was established in 1933 by the Nazi regime in Germany. It was the first song ever written in a Nazi concentration camp.

When the Nazis came to power in Germany in January 1933, Hitler's first ambition was to get back at his political opponents. Massive arrests were carried out by the SA and SS, Hitler's elite guard police. Unused factories and other facilities had to be converted into prisons to accommodate the great number of prisoners. On March 20, 1933, the first concentration camps, Oranienburg and Dachau, came into existence; others, like Börgermoor, were established in the same year. These camps were filled with members of political groups that had fought the rise of the Nazi party.

These strongly motivated political prisoners immediately organized themselves into resistance groups, and at first unrest was rife. To counteract this situation, criminal prisoners were brought into the concentration camps from maximum-security prisons. These murderers, rapists, and pathological sadists were appointed by the SS as elders or "Kapos" in the concentration camp housing units, spying, threatening, blackmailing, and in general terrorizing the other prisoners.

The treatment of the political prisoners by the SA and SS consisted of continual psychological and physical debasement. They were constantly punished with little or no provocation. If a political prisoner happened to be Jewish, his fate was twice as hard. Some were beaten to death, others were held under water until they drowned. To beings robbed of self-confidence and human dignity, physically weakened by deprivation, organized revolt became virtually impossible.

The only possible form of resistance was spiritual. Poetry and songs were written and secretly passed around to all receptive prisoners. A weekly cultural evening was initiated and everyone was urged to create something suitable for presentation.

In keeping with an old German military tradition, prisoners were forced to sing while marching to and from work. In the concentration camps only Nazi soldier songs were allowed, but prisoners began to write their own marching songs. Eventually each camp had its own song. The most famous of them was "Moorsoldaten," created in the summer of 1933 in Börgermoor, where prisoners were used to dry out peat bog swamps.

92

In response to a particularly vicious assault on the inmates by drunken SS men, one of the prisoners, a miner by the name of Esser, wrote a poem that described the desolate scenery of the swamp camp. Esser showed his poem to another prisoner, Wolfgang Langhoff, a well-known literary figure. Langhoff liked it, and with a little editing completed the text, which was then given a setting for four-part chorus by Rudi Goguel, a composer. "Moorsoldaten" was then performed, to great acclaim, at the principal cultural event of the camp, called *Zirkus Konzentrani*. The performers sang the song as they walked into the "circus arena" with their spades on their shoulders. As they sang the last lines of the song, "And then the peat bog soldiers/Won't go marching with their spades/To the bog!" the prisoners dramatically dug their spades into the ground and left without them. At the first performance, the prisoner audience spontaneously and enthusiastically sang along in the last verse. Even the SS guards joined in. "Moorsoldaten" was declared the official camp song of Börgermoor. It has also become known as "Börgermoorlied" (Song of Börgermoor).

"Moorsoldaten" soon spread to other camps; it found its way outside Germany for the first time through Erich Mirek, a prisoner at Oranienburg who was released in the summer of 1934. (Before the war, it was not unusual for even Jewish prisoners to be released from camps. The Germans did not mind the spreading of reports of their concentration camp methods. In fact, these horrifying accounts by released prisoners helped the Nazis to intimidate the populations; they served as warnings to anyone opposing the Nazi system.) As soon as he was free, Mirek went to Prague, where he sang the song to the German emigrant community.

Wolfgang Langhoff was also released from Börgermoor in 1934. He went to Paris, where in 1935 he published the book, *Moorsoldaten*, hoping through its accounts of the concentration camps to alert the world to the true nature of fascism. But only a small group listened; most of the world remained incredulous or indifferent.

The "Moorsoldaten" song also appeared in a Prague workers' newspaper on August 3, 1935. Prague was still the major city of a free, democratic Czechoslovakia. In London, the musician Hans Eissler, a German-Jewish socialist emigrant, reworked the song, and the singer Ernst Busch popularized it in the Eissler version. The song printed here, however, is the original version as it was sung by the prisoners in Börgermoor.

"Moorsoldaten" was translated into countless languages and sung in every corner of the world after World War II. (The English version is known as "Peat Bog Soldiers.") It is a memorial to those Germans who for humane reasons refused to go along with the Nazi regime. These courageous few chose to follow their human instincts and join the battle of the oppressed. Many of them lost their lives as *Moorsoldaten* in the camps.

# MOORSOLDATEN
## Peat Bog Soldiers

(In German)
Words by Esser/Wolfgang Langhoff

Music by Rudi Goguel

94

zie - hen mit den Spa - ten ins Moor.
*march - ing with our spades to the bog.*

**Fine**

Moor. Dann zieh'n die Moor - sol - da - ten Nicht mehr mit dem
*bog. Then will the peat bog sol - diers March no more with their*

Spa - ten ins Moor!
*spades to the bog!*

Wohin auch das Auge blicket
Moor und Heide nur ringsum.
Vogelsang uns nicht erquicket,
Eichen stehen kahl und krumm.

*Refrain*
Wir sind die Moorsoldaten.
Und ziehen mit dem Spaten
Ins Moor.

Auf und nieder gehn die Posten—
Keiner, keiner kann hindurch.
Flucht wird nur das leben kosten—
Vielfach ist umzaunt die Burg.

*(Refrain)*

Doch für uns gibt es kein Klagen,
Ewig kann's nicht Winter sein.
Einmal werden froh wir sagen:
Heimat, du bist wieder mein!

*Refrain*
Dann zieh'n die Moorsoldaten
Nicht mehr mit dem Spaten
Ins Moor!

NOTE: The original German text contains six verses.

*Far and wide as the eye can wander*
*Heath and bog are everywhere.*
*Not a bird sings out to cheer us,*
*Oaks are standing gaunt and bare.*

Refrain
*We are the peat bog soldiers.*
*We're marching with our spades*
*To the bog.*

*Up and down the guards are pacing—*
*No one, no one can get through.*
*Flight would mean a sure death facing—*
*Guns and barbed wire greet our view.*

(Refrain)

*But for us there's no complaining,*
*Winter will in time be past.*
*One day we shall cry, rejoicing:*
*Homeland dear, you're mine at last!*

Refrain
*Then will the peat bog soldiers*
*March no more with their spades*
*To the bog!*

# ÁSÓ KAPA VÁLLAMON
## Spade and Hoe on My Shoulder

The history of the Hungarian-Jewish labor units—the Yellow Band soldiers, as they were often called because of the yellow armbands on their uniforms—is one of the least-known tragic episodes of the Holocaust.

With the enactment of Hungary's restrictive Jewish Laws of 1938, Jewish men, instead of serving in the regular army, were drafted into labor battalions called Munka-Szolgálat—MUSZ, for short. These battalions performed auxiliary services for the Hungarian army. At first, they were used to do the dirty work for the army's technical companies—repair, maintenance, and demolition work on the Hungarian borders. When Hungary declared war against Russia, joining Axis forces on the eastern front, the Jewish auxiliary units were sent to back up the Hungarian troops in the Ukraine. There they lived and worked under conditions similar to or worse than those in concentration camps, forced to clear mines, dig tank traps, build bridges and roads, and carry ammunition and explosives for miles across steep mountain ridges.

The MUSZ men were inadequately clothed for the subzero Russian winter. They were mistreated by sadistic commanders and guards and given a bare minimum to eat. About 125,000 Jewish men between the ages of eighteen and sixty were drafted into the MUSZ. Half of them died of illnesses such as typhoid fever and dysentery; others starved, froze to death, or were murdered.

Defeated, the Hungarian army withdrew from the Russian front in 1943 and evacuated some of their MUSZ units with them. En route to Hungary through Poland, these MUSZ were forced to bury victims of the massacres of Polish Jews. Guards shot everyone who lagged behind, and few of the MUSZ made it home. Those who did survive the march often arrived just in time to be deported with their families to Auschwitz when, in March 1944, the Germans occupied Hungary. After 1944, other MUSZ units were marched through Hungary to concentration camps in Austria. Chaim Gruenfeld, who was very young when he was drafted into the MUSZ and sent to the Russian front, survived one of these marches. He told me of the savage beatings his unit was subjected to by the Austrian townspeople, who lined the streets armed with sticks and spades as the skeleton wrecks of MUSZ men passed through their villages. Only a small percentage of his unit made it to their destination, the concentration camp of Mauthausen.

I learned "Ásó Kapa Vállamon" from Chaim Gruenfeld. He did not know who wrote it. Because this song expresses cautious patriotism and willingness to serve the *haza*—the fatherland—one must assume that it was composed during the early 1940s, when the units were still stationed in Hungary. Intended as a marching song to be sung in the presence of hostile guards, it could not express anything but loyalty to the fatherland regardless of the real feelings of the men in this humiliating situation.

* * *

Both my older brothers had to serve in MUSZ units. Eugene, the elder of the two, was stationed near Budapest and labored for years in a military warehouse on the outskirts of the city. He survived the war.

Samuel, the second brother, escaped from the MUSZ and, although he was dark and looked Jewish, lived with false Aryan identity papers in Budapest. He and his roommate, another young Jew, passed as Aryans in order to help people who were in hiding, supplying them with food and medicine. Day and night Samuel worked, bringing messages, letters, and solace to these isolated people. He was betrayed to the Hungarian Gestapo and killed just one month before Budapest was liberated from the Germans by the Russian army. "If we knew where your brother's grave was, we would place flowers on it daily," I was told after the war by people whom my brother had helped during the most dangerous time. Ironically, Samuel might have been saved had his roommate telephoned him immediately after having been warned about their betrayal. Instead he ran to safety while my brother was picked up by the Gestapo, never to be seen again.

* * *

The Hungarian-Jewish poet Miklos Radnoti served in the MUSZ camp of Bor in German-occupied Serbia. During his internment, he wrote poetry that mirrors the pain and humiliation of the Yellow Band soldiers' existence. Radnoti witnessed the murders of many of his colleagues and wove his poetry around their senseless deaths. He himself was eventually killed when the Bor camp was dissolved and two thousand men were massacred.

One of Radnoti's last poems ends:

Death has given a different perspective to the past.
They sit at our tables, hide in the smiles of women, and drink from our glasses,
Those who, unburied, sleep in distant forests and foreign pastures.

# ÁSÓ KAPA VÁLLAMON
## Spade and Hoe on My Shoulder

(In Hungarian)
Author unknown

Á - só, ka - pa vál - la - mon,
*Spade and hoe on my shoul - der,*

Szi - vem - ben a bá - na - tom. Ha ve - szély - ben
*In my heart sor - rows smoul - der. When dan - ger's at our*

a ha - tár, Mun - kás szá - zad ké - szen áll, les - ben áll.
*bor - der The La - bor Com - pa - ny waits,_____ guards the gates. The*

99

Nem so - ká - ra ri - a - dó-ra fuj a kür-tös, hon - vé - dek in - du - lunk
*hour    of  a-larm  will    sound____ ral-ly 'round.__ Sol-diers,  be sure we're pre-*

**1.**
már.
*pared.*

**2.**
nap!
*rays!*

Ásó kapa vállamon,
Szivemben a bánatom.
Ha veszélyben a határ
Munkás század készen áll, lesben áll.
Nem sokára riadóra fuj a kürtös,
Honvédek indulunk már.

Zsidó szivvel dolgozunk,
Jóban, rosszban osztozunk.
Szebb napokra készülünk,
A Jo-Isten van velünk, lesz velünk.
Emelt fővel megujuló szent erővel
Hisszük hogy felsüt a nap!

*Spade and hoe on my shoulder,*
*In my heart sorrows smolder.*
*When danger's at our border*
*The Labor Company waits, guards the gates.*
*The hour of alarm will sound—rally 'round.*
*Soldiers, be sure we're prepared.*

*We work with a Jewish heart,*
*In good and bad taking part,*
*Preparing for better days.*
*The good Lord's been with us, will be with us.*
*With heads held high, on God's strength rely.*
*We await the sun's bright rays!*

# IN KRIUVKE
## In a Hideout

Many Jews, in an attempt to escape Nazi deportation, went into hiding and disappeared from view. Some found refuge in camouflaged corners of attics and cellars in the homes of non-Jewish friends. It took a great deal of courage to hide a Jew, for such acts were punished by imprisonment, deportation, even death. There were farmers in remote villages who were ready to hide Jews in dugouts under their barns and sheds for a negotiated fee. These hiding places were often so small that one could not stand up or stretch one's legs. Jews in such hideouts might not see daylight for months or even years. They lived in constant fear, especially when their money ran out, for the Germans offered tempting rewards to anyone turning in a Jew.

Once trapped in a ghetto, chances of escape were very slim, but when the ghetto dwellers realized the Nazis' intention to exterminate the Jews, many of them secretly began to dig caves and tunnels. Some of these underground hideouts were quite elaborate, with electric lights, plumbing, connecting entrances to other catacombs, and even secret exits to the outside world. Most, however, were primitive and lacked even rudimentary facilities.

The greatest hardships were endured by those Jews who ran off into the woods to hide in ditches they dug for themselves and covered only with leaves and branches. Their chance for survival was one in a hundred. German soldiers conducted systematic searches, using dogs to flush out Jews hidden in the forests. Unable to withstand the solitude, the hunger, the cold, and the fear of discovery, these fugitives often returned in despair to the ghetto.

*Kriuvka* is the Polish word for "dugout." The song "In Kriuvke," by Elia Magid and David Gertsman, was created in such a hideout in the Voronetz forest near Mezritz.

Elia Magid, a tailor, was drafted into the Polish army when the war broke out. Taken prisoner by the Germans, he was sent to a Polish prisoner-of-war camp. Soon the Germans started to kill the Jews among their prisoners. Magid managed to run away, ultimately reaching the town of Mezritz, where he entered the ghetto. He and other Jews there worked in a brush factory owned by a German and were protected for a while from deportation.

Later, ordered to be "relocated," the Jews were put on a train whose destination was the death camp of Treblinka. Magid and a few others jumped off the train and escaped into the woods at Voronetz. There they dug an underground shelter and learned to survive in the woods.

David Gertsman, like Magid a Polish soldier who had escaped from a German prisoner-of-war camp, came to share the Voronetz forest bunker with Magid and his fellow escapees. During the night the fugitives crawled out of their dugouts to search for food, eating anything even remotely edible—berries, weeds, grasses. They hunted small animals and acquired food by stealth and cunning. Often they used imitation guns carved of wood to frighten the nearby farmers into giving them food. There is a reference to this in the second verse of the song: "Now I'm an outcast in the woods . . ." The long days and nights, the insufferably slow pace of their underground existence, their fear, their sorrow, their longing for life, are all expressed in the song.

I was unable to learn anything about Gertsman's whereabouts after the war. Elia Magid survived and originally wished to remain in Poland. In July 1946, a pogrom incited by rumors of ritual murders took place in Kielce, southeastern Poland. Magid, like many other survivors, at this point decided to leave Poland for good. On a train after a farewell visit to Mezritz, he was attacked by a group of anti-Semitic Polish hoodlums, who threw all the Jews they could find out of the moving railway car. Both of Magid's legs were severed by the wheels of the train. Forced to abandon his plans for emigration, he settled in Lublin.

Anti-Semitic outbursts such as the Kielce pogrom and other expressions of hatred of the Jews were frequent occurrences in postwar Poland, a tragic aftermath for the surviving Jews. The humane gentiles who had helped the Jews during the war were discriminated against and ostracized. Many of them lost their jobs and could not find new ones. These "righteous gentiles," as they came to be known, were invited in the postwar years to Israel and other countries, where they were honored for their self-sacrificing humanitarianism.

# IN KRIUVKE

## In a Hideout

Words by Elia Magid and David Gertsman
After a Yiddish folksong

Ikh zits mir in kri-uv-ke un ikh
*In a for-est hide-out dark and*

trakht zikh, Ikh bin shoyn mid az dos oyg far-makht zikh.
*deep,___ My wea-ry eyes close but I can-not sleep.___*

Ikh bin geb-libn a-leyn, Ikh ba-gis zikh mit ge-veyn, Tsi
*I sit and wait and brood, I___ cry___ bit-ter-ly. Will we*

ve - In mir fun da - nen a - roys - geyn?
*ev - er es - cape, a - gain be free?*
Shpilt, shpilt,
*Play, play, (on)*

stru - nes fun payn,
*strings of pain,*
Shpilt-zhe mir a yi - di - shn ni - gn.
*A Yid - dish mel - o - dy please strum for me.*

Shpilt, shpilt,
*Play, play,*
stru - nes fun payn,
*(on) strings of pain,*
Tsi ve - In mir der - le - bn dem
*Will a world of peace ev - er*

fri - dn?
*be?*
Ah.

Fine
*(Echo)*

Ikh zits mir in kriuvke un ikh trakht zikh,
Ikh bin shoyn mid az dos oyg farmakht zikh.
Ikh bin geblibn aleyn, ikh bagis zikh mit geveyn,
Tsi veln mir fun danen aroysgeyn?

*Refrain*
Shpilt, shpilt, strunes fun payn—
Shpilt-zhe mir a yidishn nign.
Shpilt, shpilt, strunes fun payn—
Tsi veln mir derlebn dem fridn?

Ikh hob gelebt in hofnung un in strebn.
Ikh bin nokh yung—es velt zikh mir nokh lebn.
Geven zenen mir ruik in der heym;
Itst bin ikh a bandit in vald aleyn.

*(Refrain)*

Mir zaynen a folk fun moykhes,
Fun tsores hobn mir shoyn nit keyn koykhes.
A yedn folk iz gut, es gist nor yidish blut—
Oy, helf undz Got in itstiker minut!

*(Refrain)*

*In a forest hideout, dark and deep,*
*My weary eyes close but I cannot sleep.*
*I sit and wait and brood; I cry bitterly.*
*Will we ever escape, again be free?*

Refrain
*Play, play, strings of pain—*
*A Yiddish melody please strum for me.*
*Play, play, strings of pain—*
*Will a world of peace ever be?*

*I lived a hopeful life with much to give.*
*I am still young—I want so much to live.*
*Quietly we lived in our peaceful home;*
*Now I'm an outcast in the woods, alone.*

*(Refrain)*

*We are a people hopeful for tomorrow,*
*But now too weary to bear so much sorrow.*
*No other people suffers, only Jews they kill—*
*Oh, help us God, now, let it be thy will!*

*(Refrain)*

# TREBLINKE

Some of Treblinka's survivors called it the "hell of hells"; some referred to it as a slaughterhouse for people, overshadowing even Auschwitz, Belzets, and Maidanek in barbarism carried out with coldblooded efficiency.

Treblinka, about sixty kilometers east of Warsaw, had been a penal camp since 1941; the death camp was built between March and May of 1942. It was conceived in almost ritualistic secrecy by high-level SS staff members under Himmler's personal supervision, and designed to be the place where the final solution, the extermination of the Jews, could be realized. Not one person deported to Treblinka was supposed ever to leave it, alive or dead.

Early reports of the existence of Treblinka met with horrified disbelief. Liove Friedman, in his *Zamelbukh, Mezritz,* a memorial history of the Mezritz Jews, tells of one such early account. The two sons of Hershl Tshenki, who had been deported to Treblinka, were forced to sort out the clothing of those killed there and load the bundles into empty railroad cars. Hiding under the massive piles, they remained on one of the cars that were headed out of Treblinka and jumped from the moving train at a safe distance from the camp. Somehow they managed to return to the Mezritz ghetto, where they described the extermination procedures they had seen in Treblinka. The entire ghetto was in an uproar over the story, and most people refused to believe it. Evidently someone reported the matter to the Germans, for the two brothers were arrested and, in the presence of the *Judenaeltester* (head of the Jewish council), forced to sign a document stating that all they had said about the transports was a lie. They were then taken to the marketplace and shot.

The first time I heard about Treblinka was in a slave labor camp at Peterswaldau, near Breslau, where my sister and I had been taken from Auschwitz in August 1944. We were among a group of seventy-five girls selected for transportation to that camp in Upper Silesia, to join about eight hundred Polish Jews who were working there in a German ammunition factory. These girls had been in different ghettos and concentration camps before Peterswaldau, and some already knew of the existence of Treblinka. It was they who sang the "Treblinke" song. I can still recall the ominous awareness that the song conveyed as we listened to it in the midst of our own misery and deprivation, little though we then knew about the horrifying details of that death camp.

It is not known when or where the song "Treblinke" was written, but testimonies of the camp's escapees provide ample explanation of its details. The *umshlagplatz* mentioned in the song refers to the place where Jews were ordered to gather with their belongings for the "resettlement" transports. For one Polish zloty, the Jews were promised an entire loaf of bread for the "relocation" trip. The starved Jews rushed to register. This was a subterfuge used frequently by the Germans to learn how many Jews were in an area, and to obtain their cooperation in their deportation. The Jews were then packed into cattle cars, from eighty to one hundred twenty in each car. Only three loaves of bread were actually provided per car.

The transports were taken to Malkinia, the nearest train station to Treblinka. There, the SS guards who had accompanied the group turned it over to the specially trained SS and Ukrainian volunteers who were in charge of the death camp. Only these units were permitted beyond the camp gates. Even German airplanes were forbidden to fly over this territory.

When the cattle car doors were opened, hundreds of people fell out dead, having suffocated during the trip in the windowless wagons where they had been without food or water for days. The screams of women and children and the barking of attack dogs made such a horrible din at the arrival of each transport train that the population of the nearby village of Wulka would flee to the forest.

From each transport, one hundred fifty men were selected to cut the women's hair (it was used by the Germans for mattress stuffing) and to sort through the victims' belongings. These inmates, who were also in charge of carrying corpses to the burial pits, were periodically gassed themselves and new men were selected to replace them. After all the Jews were stripped and shaved, they were pushed into the gas chambers, the process speeded up by biting dogs, rifle butts, and kicking boots. When the transport was large, children were just thrown over the heads of the women into the gas chambers and the doors tightly sealed. At the earlier stages of the camp, the victims were asphyxiated by the fumes of running diesel engines. Later, Zyklon B was used for the gassings.

At Treblinka there were other murder methods than gassing carried out by the specially trained, usually drunken SS. "It was a luxury to die from a bullet," said an escapee, a Warsaw carpenter named Max Levitt, who was shot into a pit and lay wounded under the dead. While in the pit, he heard someone beg, "Mister guard, you did not hit me. Please shoot again." In the darkness of the night, Levitt managed to crawl out of the pit and escape. He was among the few survivors of Treblinka.

A suicidal revolt at Treblinka on August 2, 1943, was organized by Dr. Leichert, a former captain in the Polish army, and Dr. Galewski, a construction engineer. Knowing that they could not possibly win, but feeling that death in battle would be preferable to the tortures of Treblinka, the inmates determined to destroy the place before they themselves died. At unimaginable risk, they gathered knives and axes and concealed these pitiful weapons in their barracks. They also dug an underground passage to the German arsenal, where they stole hand grenades, machine guns, and pistols, hiding them in spaces under their barracks.

On the day planned for the revolt, a hot August day, some of the Ukrainian watchtower guards had gone for a swim. The Jews seized the guards' machine guns. Hand grenades were exploded; gasoline was poured on the barracks, storehouses, and gas chambers, which were then set on fire. Soon Treblinka was ablaze.

The battle went on for six hours, but heavy reinforcements came to the Germans from all directions and the rebels were massacred. About forty escaped into the woods, evading the Germans' exhaustive search. The leaders, the heroic Dr. Leichert and Dr. Galewski, lost their lives in the battle, but their aim was accomplished, for the Germans blew up whatever was left of the camp after the revolt. The site of the mass graves was cleared and leveled, and pine trees were planted over the entire area.

From May 1942 to August 1943, more than ten thousand Jews were killed *daily* in Treblinka. In all, there were only seventy survivors, many of whom have already passed away. The song "Treblinke" remains to honor the memory of all who there met their death.

# TREBLINKE

Author unknown

hert men a ge-shray
*hears a scream of pain*

Vi eyn kind veynt tsu der ma-men:_
*As a child cries to its moth-er,___*

"Ge-lozt hos-tu mikh gants a-leyn,__
*"I'm a-fraid here on this wag-on train:___*

'Kh'vil blay - bn mit dir tsu-
*I want to stay with you to-*

**1.2.**

za-men!"
*geth-er."___*

**Fine**

In toyt.___
*we'd meet.___*

Kum tsu-rik, tsu-rik mayn ma-me-nyu.
*Come back, come back, my dear-est ma-me-nyu.*

Come

Kum, akh kum, tsu-rik tsu mir. Kum tsu-rik, tsu-rik mayn
*back, oh please come back to me. Come back, come back, my dear-est*

ma-me-nyu, Di gan-tse tsayt bin ikh ge-ven mit dir, Treb-lin-ke
*ma-me-nyu, Why can't it be the way it used to be? Treb-lin-ka*

dorf,_____ Fun a-le Yi-dn gi-ter ort._____
*there,_____ Grave-yard of Jews from ev-'ry - where._____*

Ver s'kumt a-hin der blaybt shoyn dort, Der blaybt shoyn ey-bik dort.
*Who ev-er is sent re-mains_____ there, For ev-er, ev-er there.*

Ver s'kumt a - hin
*All who come there*

Fun bri - der, shves-ter, ta - tes,
*Young-sters, eld - ers, fa-thers,*

ma - men,—
*moth-ers,—*

Un dor-tn tut men zey far - tsa-men—
*All my dear-est sis-ters, broth-ers,—*

Un dort iz zey - er sof.
*And there they meet their death.*

Dort nit vayt fun dorf,
Dort iz der umshlagplatz geleygt,
Dort vu men shtipt zikh in di breyt
In di vagonen arayn.
Un dortn hert men a geshray
Vi eyn kind veynt tsu der mamen:
"Gelozt hostu mikh gants aleyn,
Kh'vil blaybn mit dir tsuzamen!"

Di yidishe politsay,
Zi hot geheysn shneller geyn:
"Ir vet nit visn fun keyn noyt,
Ir vet bakumen tsu esn broyt."
Un azoy hobn zey uns farnart,
Az mir vern bakum'n tsu esn broyt...
Un keyner fun uns hot nit gegloybt
In Treblinke den shneln toyt.

Kum tsurik, tsurik, mayn mamenyu,
Kum, akh kum, tsurik tsu mir.
Kum tsurik, tsurik, mayn mamenyu,
Di gantse tsayt bin ikh geven mit dir!

Treblinke dorf,
Fun ale yidn guter ort,
Ver s'kumt ahin der blaybt shoyn dort,
Der blaybt oyf eybik dort.
Ver s'kumt ahin
Fun brider, shvester, tates, mamen,
Un dortn tut men zey fartsamen
Un dort iz zeyer sof.

There, outside the town,
They gather Jews from near and far,
With blows and curses they are massed
In crowded cattle cars.
And there one hears a scream of pain
As a child cries to its mother,
"I'm afraid here on this wagon train,
I want to stay with you together."

"Go faster! Hurry! Faster!"
At us the Jewish police yell.
"You'll all be cared for and well fed,
To each a whole loaf of bread."
And so have we all been deceived
That we'd all have some bread to eat...
And none of us really believed
In Treblinka death we'd meet.

Come back, come back, my dearest mamenyu,
Come back, oh please come back to me.
Come back, come back, my dearest mamenyu.
Why can't it be the way it used to be?

Treblinka there—
Graveyard of Jews from everywhere.
Whoever is sent remains there
For ever, ever there.
All who come there—
Youngsters, elders, fathers, mothers,
All my dearest sisters, brothers—
And there they meet their death.

# SHTILER, SHTILER
## Quiet, Quiet

Vilna has been called by poets the "Jerusalem of Lithuania," for it was a major center of spiritual and cultural life for Eastern European Jewry before the war. A fertile soil for opposing religious sects such as the Khassidim and Mitnagdim, the city also spawned the most important Jewish labor and pioneering Zionist (Khalutsic) movements. Many notable personalities of Jewish life—rabbis, preachers, scholars, cantors, artists, musicians, and theatrical people—came from Vilna.

During World War II, despite the daily horrors of the Nazi occupation, cultural life among Vilna's Jews did not die. "Our bodies may be enslaved, but our souls are not," was the guiding principle in the Vilna ghetto. Unable to protect their physical beings, Vilna's Jews nurtured their spirit with poetry readings, lectures, literary discussions, and music.

Some of the best-known ghetto songs originated in the Vilna ghetto and were carried to concentration and slave labor camps by those deported from there. "Shtiler, Shtiler," perhaps the most famous of all ghetto songs, was written in Vilna in the spring of 1943. At that time, news of Allied victories began to spread and, with renewed hopes for an end of the war, there was a wave of creativity among the ghetto dwellers. In April, the Literary Artistic Circle launched a musical competition. The prizes were extra rations of bread, sugar, or eggs. An eleven-year-old boy, Alec Volkoviski, won the first prize with a moving composition. The poet Shmerke Kaczerginski later wrote words to this piece, and thus "Shtiler, Shtiler" was created. The song begins with the line "Quiet, quiet, let's be silent,/Graves are growing here," and proceeds to recount the tragedy of Ponar.

Ponar—Ponary in Polish—was to the Vilna ghetto people what Babi Yar was to the Kiev Jews: A nearby wooded area, it had been a favorite rustic place for recreation and weekend outings. During the Nazi occupation, it was a place of death. When the Germans occupied Vilna in 1941, Ponar had been deleted from their official maps of the area, for they had exact plans for that place. It was used as an execution and burial site for victims of the roundups and night raids. Close to eighty thousand people were massacred in the pits of Ponar between 1941 and 1944. Dead bodies were thrown into two huge pits which the Russians, who occupied Vilna before the Germans, had dug for the storage of petrol tanks.

After a while the pits became inadequate, and it was necessary to burn the victims instead of just burying them. Squadrons of ghetto prisoners were brought in to do the job.

114

In "Shtiler, Shtiler," Kaczerginski, inspired by the sad tune that sprang from the suffering of the child composer, gives voice to the pain of a woman whose husband had been taken to Ponar. She soothes her child by saying that his father will come back, though she knows that the roads to Ponar, on which he disappeared, permit no return. The poem also expresses love for a once peaceful Vilna, with its beautiful river Vilya, now enslaved by winter's ice, just as its people are enslaved by the enemy's oppression. In the third and last verse of the song, the mother, through her love, sees freedom's reflection in her child's face.

Normally, it takes a long time before a composed song becomes part of the folklore, but in the ghettos folklore was created instantaneously with songs like "Shtiler, Shtiler." Since the Germans forbade mention of Ponar in the ghetto, the text of "Shtiler, Shtiler" had to be changed whenever it was sung aloud, but everyone knew the true meaning of the song, and its popularity was enormous.

Alec Volkoviski survived the war in the concentration camp to which he was taken with his mother after the liquidation of the Vilna ghetto. He settled in Israel after the war. Like the father in the song, however, his own father, Dr. Noakh Volkoviski, perished during the Holocaust.

# SHTILER, SHTILER
## Quiet, Quiet

Words by Shmerke Kaczerginski

Music by Alec Volkoviski

Shti - ler, shti - ler, lo - mir shvay-gn, Kvo - rim vak - sn do.
*Qui - et, qui - et, let's be si - lent, Graves are grow-ing here.*

S'ho - bn zey far - flantst di so - nim: Gri - nen zey tsum blo.
*Plant - ed cruel - ly by the ene - my: Sky - ward grows the bier.*

S'fi – rn ve – gn tsu Po – nar tsu, S'firt keyn veg tsu – rik.
*All roads seem to lead to Po – nar, None of them re – turns. That's*

Iz der ta – te vu far-shvun – dn, Un mit im dos glick.
*where your fa – ther dis-ap-peared; With sor – row my heart yearns.*

Shti – ler, kind mayns, veyn nit, oyt – ser, S'helft nit keyn ge – veyn.
*Qui – et, lit-tle one, don't cry, treas-ure, What use are your tears?*

Un – dzer um – glick ve – In so – nim Say vi nit far-shteyn.
*To our cries the heart-less ene – my Turns its cold deaf ears.*

S'ho - bn bre - ges oykh di ya - men, S'ho - bn tfi - ses oy - khet tsa - men.
*E - ven o - ceans have their shore - lines, Lim - it - ed are pris - on grounds.*

Nor tsu un - dzer payn Keyn bi - sl shayn._____ Keyn bi - sl
*On - ly our pain, our end - less sor - row, Has_____ no bounds, no*

shayn.
*bounds.*

rit. e dim.

| | |
|---|---|
| Shtiler, shtiler, lomir shvaygn,<br>Kvorim vaksn do.<br>S'hobn zey farflantst di sonim:<br>Grinen zey tsum blo.<br>S'firn vegn tsu Ponar tsu,<br>S'firt keyn veg tsurik.<br>Iz der tate vu farshvundn—<br>Un mit im dos glik.<br>Shtiler, kind mayns, veyn nit, oytser,<br>S'helft nit keyn geveyn.<br>Undzer umglik veln sonim<br>Say vi nit farshteyn.<br>S'hobn breges oykh di yamen,<br>S'hobn tfises oykhet tsamen.<br>Nor tsu undzer payn<br>Keyn bisl shayn. Keyn bisl shayn. | *Quiet, quiet, let's be silent,*<br>*Graves are growing here.*<br>*Planted cruelly by the enemy:*<br>*Skyward grows the bier.*<br>*All roads seem to lead to Ponar,*<br>*None of them returns.*<br>*That's where your father disappeared—*<br>*With sorrow my heart yearns.*<br>*Quiet, little one, don't cry, treasure,*<br>*What use are your tears?*<br>*To our cries the heartless enemy*<br>*Turns its cold deaf ears.*<br>*Even oceans have their shorelines,*<br>*Limited are prison grounds.*<br>*Only our pain, our endless sorrow,*<br>*Has no bounds, no bounds.* |
| Friling oyfn land gekumen<br>Un undz harbst gebrakht.<br>Iz der tog haynt ful mit blumen—<br>Undz zet nor di nakht.<br>Goldikt shoyn der harbst oyf shtamen—<br>Blit in undz der tsar.<br>Blaybt faryosemt vu a mame—<br>S'kind geyt oyf Ponar.<br>Vi di Vilye a geshmidte,<br>T'oykh geyokht in payn,<br>Tsien kries ayz durkh lite<br>Itst in yam arayn.<br>S'vert der khoyshekh vu tserunen,<br>Fun der fintster laykhtn zunen.<br>Rayter, kum geshvind—<br>Dikh ruft dayn kind. Dikh ruft dayn kind. | *When Spring came this year to our land,*<br>*For us it brought bleak fall.*<br>*Days may still be full of flowers—*<br>*We have night's dark pall.*<br>*Fall turns leafy branches golden—*<br>*In us grows deep pain.*<br>*They take the mother's child to Ponar—*<br>*Her tears are all in vain.*<br>*Enslaved like the River Vilya,*<br>*Kept from ocean shores,*<br>*Dragged by ice blocks through Lithuania*<br>*Into frozen moors.*<br>*The darkness must someday vanish,*<br>*The bright gold sunshine will come through.*<br>*Hurry, rider, come—*<br>*Your child calls you, your child calls you.* |
| Shtiler, shtiler, s'kveln kvaln<br>Undz in harts arum.<br>Biz der toyer vet nit faln<br>Zayn mir muzn shtum.<br>Frey nit, kind, zikh, s'iz dayn shmeykhl,<br>Itst far undz farrat.<br>Zen dem friling zol der soyne<br>Vi in harbst a blat.<br>Zol der kval zikh ruik flisn,<br>Shtiler zay un hof.<br>Mit der frayheyt kumt der tate—<br>Shlof zhe, kind mayn, shlof.<br>Vi di Vilye a bafrayte,<br>Vi di beymer grin-banayte,<br>Laykht bald frayheyts-likht<br>Oyf dayn gezikht. Oyf dayn gezikht. | *Quiet, quiet, growing anguish,*<br>*Hearts in agony.*<br>*Till the ghetto gates have fallen*<br>*We must silent be.*<br>*Hide your gladness, hide your smile,*<br>*Our hope we'll not betray.*<br>*Let the enemy see our springtime*<br>*Like a bleak fall day.*<br>*Let the pain flow still as moonglow,*<br>*Hope in silence keep.*<br>*Liberty will bring your papa—*<br>*Sleep, my darling, sleep.*<br>*Like the river freely flowing,*<br>*Like tall trees with new green glowing,*<br>*Freedom's light will grace*<br>*Your dear sweet face, your dear sweet face.* |

# DREMLEN FEYGL
## Birds Are Dreaming

"Dremlen Feygl," a lullaby from the Vilna ghetto, stirs such deep feelings of grief in a singer that despite its simplicity it is very difficult to perform. In the three short verses of this beautiful song, the entire tragedy of the destruction of Jewish life by the Nazis unfolds. It tells of the fate of one of the countless children left orphaned after each roundup in the ghetto.

Lea Rudnitska, a young teacher and poet of the Vilna ghetto, took such a child into her home. Soothing the child to sleep, she conceived the text of "Dremlen Feygl," imagining the happiness that once surrounded the cradle of the now motherless and fatherless child.

Lea Rudnitska was born in 1916 in the little Lithuanian town of Kalvarie, near Kovno. She moved to Vilna in 1939, when the war broke out. Her poetry and other writings were already known and appreciated, having been published in various Jewish papers. In 1940, when Vilna was under Russian occupation, she joined the staff of *Vilna Emes*—Vilna Truth—a Yiddish journal edited by young writers and poets. The sudden takeover of Vilna by the Germans in 1941, and the subsequent rapid ghettoization of the Jewish community, clouded the young woman's spirit, and her poems became filled with sorrow and pain. She aptly entitled a small volume of her poetry from that time *Neplen* (Fogs).

In the ghetto, Rudnitska was put in charge of a sewing workshop. Among the women in the shop was Pesye Aronowicz, the first person to have escaped from the ditches of Ponar. Under cover of darkness, though wounded, Pesye had managed to return to the ghetto, leaving her two small children behind her, dead, in the pit. To avoid panic, the ghetto's Jewish authorities decided to keep her experiences secret. Very few people learned the truth of these first Ponar massacres. Lea Rudnitska was one of them.

Despite many obstacles, Rudnitska was among the most active participants in the ghetto's cultural life. Musicians, artists, writers, and poets formed the Literary Artistic Circle, which met every week or two for lectures, discussions, and readings of the classics as well as of original works created in the ghetto. The subjects of these intellectually demanding evenings were diverse and included, aside from Jewish poetry and music, the history of Vilna, the paintings of Marc Chagall, Shakespeare's *Merchant of Venice*, Lessing's *Nathan the Wise*. Ghetto artists decorated the meeting room to make it appropriate to the subject under discussion. Prominent participants in these evenings were Jakov Gerstein, Gershon Feldman, Morris Hyman, and the guiding spirit of the

Lea Rudnitska, 1916–1943.

literary circle, Zalman Kalmanivicz. Rudnitska often read from her works at these meetings, and on at least two occasions was awarded a prize.

These evenings were of tremendous importance to their participants as a source of spiritual recovery. Dr. Mark Dworecky, a survivor of the Vilna ghetto, recalls in his book, *The Destruction of the Jerusalem of Lithuania,* that in the middle of one of these literary evenings, air raid sirens began to blow. Everyone was urged to take shelter in the basement, but not a single person was willing to leave the meeting. It was better to be killed by a bomb while engrossed in a literary discussion, they thought, than to die slowly at the hands of the Germans.

At the liquidation of the Vilna ghetto in 1943, Lea Rudnitska was selected to go "to the left," which in Nazi terms meant to be condemned to death. She was killed either in Treblinka or Maidanek.

Lea set the text of "Dremlen Feygl" to an existing tune by the Russian-Jewish composer Leyb Yampolsky.

121

# DREMLEN FEYGL
## Birds Are Dreaming

Lea Rudnitska

Moving gently

Lyu-lyu-lyu, lyu-lyu-lyu.
*Lyu-lyu-lyu, lyu-lyu-lyu.*

Drem-len fey – gl oyf di tsvay-gn, Shlof, mayn ta – yer kind.
*Birds are dream-ing on the branch-es; Sleep, the dark night brings.*

Bay dayn vi – gl, oyf dayn na – re Zitst a frem-de un zingt.
*At your cra – dle in the dug-out, A stran-ger sits and sings.*

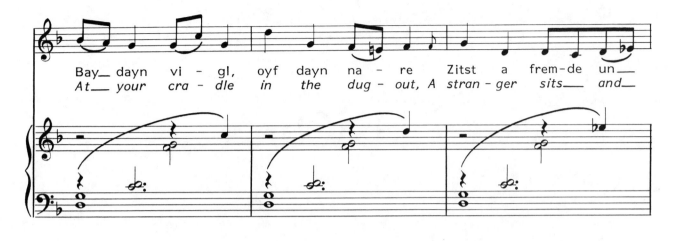

Bay__ dayn vi – gl, oyf dayn na – re Zitst a frem-de un__
*At__ your cra – dle in the dug – out, A stran – ger sits__ and__*

zingt.  Lyu-lyu-lyu,  lyu-lyu-lyu,  lyu.
*sings.  Lyu-lyu-lyu,  lyu-lyu-lyu,  lyu.*

Dremlen feygl oyf di tsvaygn,
Shlof, mayn tayer kind.
Bay dayn vigl, oyf dayn nare
Zitst a fremde un zingt.

Lyu-lyu-lyu, lyu-lyu-lyu.

S'iz dayn vigl vu geshtanen
Oysgeflokhtn fun glik,
Un dayn mame, oy dayn mame,
Kumt shoyn keynmol nit tsurik.

Lyu-lyu-lyu, lyu-lyu-lyu.

Kh'hob gezen dayn tatn loyfn
Unter hogl fun shteyn.
Iber felder iz gefloygn
Zayn faryosemter geveyn.

Lyu-lyu-lyu, lyu-lyu-lyu.

*Birds are dreaming on the branches,*
*Sleep the dark night brings.*
*At your cradle in the dugout*
*A stranger sits and sings.*

*Lyu-lyu-lyu, lyu-lyu-lyu.*

*Once you had a little cradle*
*Woven out of joy,*
*But your mama never again*
*Will see her little boy.*

*Lyu-lyu-lyu, lyu-lyu-lyu.*

*I have seen your father running*
*Under a hail of stone.*
*Over the fields sounds his sad cry,*
*Abandoned, all alone.*

*Lyu-lyu-lyu, lyu-lyu-lyu.*

# YISROLIK

Yisrolik, the hero of this song from Vilna, is a child peddler in the ghetto. A boy of eleven or twelve, he risks his life daily, sneaking outside the walls to gather food and cigarettes in the city, smuggling the forbidden goods back inside to give to his family and to sell on the ghetto streets.

How did the Yisroliks of the ghettos manage to find food, and how did they manage to sneak it past the ghetto guards? Their ways were wily and mysterious—almost magical—as they roamed the heavily guarded ghetto, skirted fortified walls and barbed-wire fences, sneaked through the sewer pipes, and mingled audaciously with the spies, policemen, Gestapo agents, and hostile citizens of the Polish-Lithuanian streets. Many of them were caught and paid with their lives, but what was that to risk? In the ghetto there was no chance of survival without contraband food, and these undersized, undernourished ghetto kids were more likely to succeed in their attempts at smuggling than were full-grown men or women.

Once on the free city streets, the ghetto dealer kids mingled with the non-Jewish

Lev Rozenthal, 1916–1944.

124

child peddlers who sang, begged, and peddled their wares on every street corner. Those who were blond and blue-eyed stood a better chance of passing as non-Jewish, though often they had to bribe the local bullies so as not to be denounced.

The young ghetto dealers' days were as arduous as they were hazardous: they had to steal cigarettes or buy them on the black market and sell them to German soldiers or Polish citizens. In payment they would accept cash or bread, potatoes or canned foods. Wearing oversized coats salvaged from junk heaps, they could hide remarkable amounts of foodstuffs in their pockets. The hard part was to sneak the food past the guards on the way back, a feat somewhat less impossible when the work crews were returning to the ghetto and when only Polish and Jewish police were on duty. Often the police had to be bribed with cigarettes or food at the ghetto gates.

As often as not, it was impossible to get back into the ghetto with the smuggled goods, and the children had to sleep outside the walls in ruins, cellars, or open fields. Occasionally, in the coldest weather, some goodhearted Polish man or woman would take pity and shelter them for a few days, but they could not often count on such benevolence.

There were literally thousands of Yisroliks in the Vilna and Warsaw ghettos during the Nazi occupation. Without them, starvation would have come even sooner to many. The bravery of these children, tough and cocky on the outside but bereaved and frightened underneath, cannot be evaluated. When the ghetto fighters organized their resistance struggle, these children served as messengers to the outside world and as smugglers of arms into the ghetto. Very few survived, for most of them were hunted down by the Germans and shot.

"Yisrolik" was the first song written on a ghetto theme in Vilna. It captures the brash defiance, the courageous moral resistance of the little hero who had no time for tears, complaints, or grief. As the song tells us, he had to be tough and keep his spirits going with a song and a whistle.

The lyrics of "Yisrolik" were written by the poet and playwright Lev Rozenthal, the music by the pianist and composer Misha Veksler. It was first performed by Khayele Rozenthal, Lev Rozenthal's sister, at the memorable concert on January 18, 1942, in the Vilna ghetto. The composer, the lyricist, and the performer were all important figures in the ghetto's cultural life. After the liquidation of the Vilna ghetto, in 1943, Lev Rozenthal was taken to the Dutmergen concentration camp, where he died. Misha Veksler, a hunchbacked cripple due to childhood polio, spent his ghetto years in hiding, for the Nazis eliminated all those with physical disabilities in the very first roundups. He composed many other popular ghetto songs in obscure hideouts. When the ghetto was liquidated, Veksler was taken to Ponar and killed. Of the three, only Khayele survived the war. After her release from the concentration camp into which she was eventually thrown, she emigrated to Capetown, South Africa.

In the song "Yisrolik," the ghetto inhabitants found the essence of Jewish survival. The name chosen for the song's protagonist is a diminutive of Yisrael—the Jewish people. Yisrolik is the tough little Jew who finds a way to survive no matter what, and thus symbolizes spiritual resistance. The courage and selflessness of the Yisroliks cannot be exaggerated. With far more generosity than may be found in most adults, they helped their families, their friends, and each other, and spread hope and courage beyond measure.

# YISROLIK

Words by Lev Rozenthal

Music by Misha Veksler

Moderato ( ♩ = 88–94)

koyft zhe pa – pi – ro – sn,   Nu koyft zhe sa – kha – rin.   Ge-
*come and buy my cig-a-rettes,*   *— Sweet-'ner and oth-er good things.*

vo – rn iz haynt skhoy-re bi – lik vert._____   A
*Try my bar-gains, I won't be un-der-bid._____*   *A*

le - bn far a gro - shn, A pru - te - a far - dinst. Fun ge - to - hend - ler
*life__ for a pen - ny, My prof - it's e - ven less. __ You must know me, the*

hot ir dokh ge - hert! _____ Kh'heys Yis - ro - lik, Ikh
*ghet - to deal - er kid! _____ I'm called Yis - ro - lik, Your*

*Refrain*

bin dos kind fun ge - to. Kh'heys Yis - ro - lik A
*kid__ from the ghet - to. I'm called Yis - ro - lik; __*

hef - ker - di - ker yung. Khotsh far - bli - bn
*Hef - ty, tough and strong. I am al - ways*

127

go - le ne - to, Der - lang ikh alts nokh, A svisht - she un a
*broke and yet, oh, can al - ways mus - ter, A whis - tle and a*

1. *Etc.* Fine (Free)

zung! zung! (Whistle or hum)
*song! song!*

Colla voce

Tsu vos der mo - nen Un ma - khn s'harts zikh shver.
*Why re - mem - ber And grieve my heav - y heart?*

128

Nu koyft zhe papirosn,
Nu koyft zhe sakharin.
Gevorn iz haynt skhoyre bilik vert.
A lebn far a groshn,
A prute-a fardinst—
Fun geto-hendler hot ir dokh gehert.

*Refrain*
Kh'heys Yisrolik—
Ikh bin dos kind fun geto.
Kh'heys Yisrolik—
A hefkerdiker yung.
Khotsh farblibn gole-neto,
Derlang ikh alts nokh
A svistshe un a zung!

A mantl on a kragn,
Takhtoynim fun a zak;
Kaloshn hob ikh—s'feln nor di shikh.
Un ver es vet nor vagn,
Tsu lakhn; oy, a sakh—
Dem vel ikh nokh vayzn ver bin ikh!

(Refrain)

Nit meynt mikh hot geborn
Di hefkerdike gas.
Bay tate-mame oykh geven a kind.
Kh'hob beydn ongevorn,
Nit meynt es iz a shpas—
Kh'bin geblibn vi in feld der vint.

*Refrain*
Kh'heys Yisrolik—
Nor ven keyner zet nit
Vish ikh shtil zikh.
Fun oyg arop a trer.
Nor fun mayn troyer—
Beser az men redt nit,
Tsu vos dermonen
Un makhn s'harts zikh shver.

So, come and buy my cigarettes,
Sweet'ner and other good things.
Try my bargains, I won't be underbid.
A life for a penny,
My profit's even less.
You must know me—the ghetto dealer kid.

Refrain
I'm called Yisrolik—
Your kid from the ghetto.
I'm called Yisrolik—
Hefty, tough, and strong.
I'm always broke and yet, oh,
I can always muster
A whistle and a song!

A coat without collar,
Pants made from a sack;
I have galoshes but no shoes inside.
No one better holler,
No one give me flak.
Don't laugh at me—you see, I have my pride!

(Refrain)

But that's not how I started
Out in this tough place.
Mother, father made me a loving home.
But now I'm brokenhearted,
It's no joke to face—
I'm left like the wind in the field, alone.

Refrain
I'm called Yisrolik—
And when no one sees me,
Quietly I wipe away a tear.
Of grief I've had my part.
Let's not talk about it—
Why remember
And grieve my heavy heart?

# TANTS, TANTS, TANTS
## Dance, Dance, Dance

In rare moments of quiet in the ghetto, when no German was around, someone who had salvaged a musical instrument would begin to play so couples could dance. Yes, sometimes they danced in the ghetto. In worn-out shoes and torn, shabby clothes, the dancers held each other tight and moved in rhythm to the soothing dance tunes, to warm their often freezing bodies and to forget for a few moments the oppression around them.

"Tants, Tants, Tants," one of the favorite songs of the Vilna ghetto, describes in an ironic, self-mocking style such a scene of ghetto dancers. The first verse of the song, which is set to a Polish wedding tune, tells of the bitter frosts in the ghetto and of fur collars torn from Jews' coats.

The Germans did not allow the Jews to wear furs in the ghetto. Even fur collars or linings were ripped off and sent to German soldiers on the Russian front. Exposing Jews to cold was, like starvation, one of the methods of the final solution.

The second stanza of the song focuses on the Judenrat, the council of Jews in charge of carrying out German commands in the ghetto. This governing body, which served as a liaison between the Jews and the Nazis, was sometimes elected by the Jews themselves and sometimes set up by the Germans. Whatever the method of selection, the council was trapped by the Nazi machinery. This was not immediately clear to all of its members, who, in the beginning, were recruited from among professionally or intellectually respected people already active in the communities. Some of these men were idealists who felt responsible for the welfare of their fellow Jews, and who volunteered to serve on the councils in the hopes of obtaining proper housing, food, schooling, etc., for the ghetto population. It soon became evident, however, that the Germans intended to use the Judenrat strictly as a tool in the preliminary work of extermination. Each day they made new and more difficult demands of this council: first the confiscation and deliverance to the Germans of all Jewish property; then the registration of every ghetto inhabitant and the submission of a list of all those incapable of forced labor (the old, the sick, the children), who were then primary targets for deportation. When their role became clear to them, some members of the Judenrat committed suicide; others took advantage of the momentary power they had in the ghetto and, through it, the possibility of saving their own and their family's lives. However, when the ghettos were liquidated, the Judenrat was not spared. Members were killed as soon as the Germans no longer needed them. Whatever their initial motivations,

Judenrat members were the targets of the mockery and contempt, at best, and of the hatred and vengeance, at worst, of the ghetto people.

"Dance, dance, dance a little bit with me./If you have a yellow paper ..." continues the song, referring to the *gele shayne*. These yellow passes (other colors were also used) were valid for a very brief time. They were necessary not only for food and firewood rations, but for survival itself, for without these identification papers one might be hunted down and sent to a death camp. The Germans distributed only a limited number of the passes, each of which could sustain up to four members of a family. There were chilling scenes when a family of more than four had to choose who among its members would survive. Many large families rejected the passes, preferring to be deported together.

Unmarried pass-owners were able to adopt or create a surrogate family and thus temporarily save them from deportation. "If you have a yellow paper/You can marry me ..." Consequently, those with passes and no families were wooed by people without passes. In the song's third stanza, a married man without a paper seems to invite a single girl who has a yellow paper to dance with him. He thinks of his wife and wonders if they'll ever be home again together.

The author of the text of this song is unknown.

# TANTS, TANTS, TANTS

## Dance, Dance, Dance

Author unknown
To A Polish Wedding Tune

Heavy

Hot zikh mir di shikh tse – ri – sn, Vey tsu may – ne yorn! Di
*My old shoes are worn and torn, Oh, woe is un – to me! They*

kra – gns hot men undz op – ge – ri – sn, Ver ikh dokh far – fro – rn!
*ripped our col – lars from our coats, How fro – zen we will be!*

132

Tants, tants, tants a bi - se - le mit mir,
Dance, dance, dance a lit - tle bit with me.

Oy, ir\_\_\_\_ groy - se fre - ste - lekh Ir kumt dokh fun Si -
frosts come\_\_\_ from Si - be - ri - a, From far a - cross the

**1. 2.**
bir.
sea.

**3.**
bir.
sea.

Ge - le shay - nen,
Yel - low pa - pers,

ro-ze shay — nen, A-ler-lay ko — li — rn Ven vel ikh mayn
*pink_ pa-pers, man-y col-ors I can see._____ When will my dear*

vai — bl Zla — te tsu zikh a-heym shoyn fi — rn? Tants, tants,
*wife, my Zla — te, Be home a-gain with me?_____ Dance, dance,*

tants a bi — se-le mit mir. Ho-stu a ge-ln
*dance a lit — tle bit with me. If you_ have a*

shayn_____ Hob ikh kha — se-ne mit dir.
*yel — low pa-per You can mar-ry me.*

Tants, tants, tants a bi - se - le mit mir.
*Dance, dance, dance a lit - tle bit with me.*

*poco a poco diminuendo*

Ah,

Ah,

Ah.

135

Hot zikh mir di shikh tserisn—
Vey tsu mayne yorn!
Di kragns hot men undz opgerisn—
Ver ikh dokh farfrorn.

*Refrain*
Tants, tants, tants
A bisele mit mir.
Oy, ir groyse frestelekh
Ir kumt dokh fun Sibir.

Broyt oyfn tsentimeter,
Holts oyfn deko,
Hot undz farzorgt der yidnrat
Der yidnrat fun geto.

*Refrain*
Tants, tants, tants
A bisele mit mir.
Hostu a geln shayn
Hob ikh khasene mit dir.

Gele shaynen, roze shaynen,
Alerley kolirn.
Ven vel ikh mayn vaybl Zlate
Tsu zikh aheym shoyn firn?

*(Refrain)*

My old shoes are worn and torn—
Oh, woe is unto me!
They ripped our collars from our coats—
How frozen we will be!

Refrain
Dance, dance, dance
A little bit with me.
Big frosts come from Siberia,
From far across the sea.

Bread they give us by the inch,
Firewood by the ounce,
The Judenrat, the ghetto police,
Was ordered to announce.

Refrain
Dance, dance, dance
A little bit with me.
If you have a yellow paper
You can marry me.

Yellow papers, pink papers,
Many colors I can see.
When will my dear wife, my Zlate,
Be home again with me?

(Refrain)

# YUGNT-HIMEN
## Hymn of Youth

Spiritual resistance in the Vilna ghetto manifested itself, as we have seen, in an enormous variety of cultural activities. Besides the Literary Artistic Circle, there were the theater and opera performances, and the concerts of symphonic and choral music, the latter performed by the ghetto's two choruses, one Yiddish and another Hebrew. Schools for children and universities with faculties in mathematics, physics and chemistry, natural history, linguistics, and social studies were conducted secretly, education being forbidden. Clearly, ghettoization did not stop the traditions of Vilna's glorious past, which had earned it a reputation as the spiritual Mecca of Eastern European Jews.

Far more complicated was the organization of physical resistance. While it was natural for the young people to ally themselves in an active fight against the oppressors, the older, more traditional people of the ghetto hoped—especially in the beginning—that compliance with German demands would prevent major trouble, and they opposed actual fighting. Unwilling or unable to give credence to first reports of the systematic murder being carried out under their very noses, they tried to curb the younger, more volatile Jews among them. Even when those few who escaped the mass killings managed to get back to the ghettos, most people refused to believe their accounts of the killing grounds; as far as was possible, the stories were suppressed to prevent panic. There are reports of mothers who bound their very young children to their beds so that they could not escape to the forests to join the partisans. "The family stays together in good and in bad" was the still vital principle of Jewish tradition.

Nevertheless, resistance groups were organized by the young, and on October 24, 1941, an active rebellion, the first ever to occur in a ghetto, began in Vilna. Twenty-five young Jews barricaded themselves in a cellar and fought an hour-long battle, wounding or killing several Germans. From then on, there was constant underground activity, involving the procuring of guns and ammunition outside the ghetto for future use by resistance fighters. In January 1942, the Fareynigte Partisaner Organizatsie, or FPO—Unified Fighting Organization—was created, with the legendary Yitskhak Vitenberg as its leader. At first, the FPO planned to fight from within the ghetto rather than escape to the partisans in the forests. Tragically, Vitenberg was betrayed and had to give himself up to the Germans to avoid the massacre of the entire ghetto.

Shmerke Kaczerginski, the author of "Shtiler, Shtiler" and "Varshe," wrote "Yugnt-Himen" for the Yugnt-Club—Youth Club—the ghetto organization designed to give teenagers an opportunity to learn, to practice sports, and to help each other endure. Composed at a time when spirits were particularly low, and the young badly needed

Shmerke Kaczerginski, 1908–1954, as a partisan fighter against the Nazis. He seems to be holding his automatic rifle the way he had held his guitar.

hope and encouragement, the song was adopted by young and old for its assertion that "Young is every one of us who wants it that way," as the chorus emphatically repeats. The Youth Club sang their hymn with special fervor at every meeting. In 1943, when the majority of the clandestine ghetto fighters moved into the forests, many of the members of the Youth Club, some of them no more than thirteen or fourteen years old, went with them.

"Yugnt-Himen" became immensely popular in the ghettos and remains well known even today. Shmerke Kaczerginski, the author of its stirring lyrics, was one of the fine young people of prewar Vilna who grew up with high expectations in that culturally fertile Jewish environment. Like so many others, he had his youth violently interrupted by the German invasion of Poland and the subsequent Nazi occupation.

Born in 1908 to impoverished parents who died of hunger during World War I, Shmerke and his younger brother were raised by their paternal grandparents. He attended evening classes while doing his apprenticeship as a lithographer. An active member of the literary club Yung Vilna, he began while still very young to write stories about the life of workingmen in Poland.

During World War II, Kaczerginski played an important role in the cultural and educational life of the ghetto. Even more vital was his involvement in the ghetto's secret resistance organization. By the time the ghetto was liquidated, in 1943, many of the resistance fighters had managed to join the partisans in the surrounding forests. For the last two years of the war, Kaczerginski fought with his unit in the Narotsh forest, an area about ninety kilometers from Vilna.

The music to "Yugnt-Himen" was written by Basya Rubin, a woman of the Vilna ghetto who survived the war in a concentration camp and then emigrated to Israel.

# YUGNT-HIMEN
## Hymn of Youth

Words by Shmerke Kaczerginski

Music by Basya Rubin

yu - gnt     mit ge-zang.     Yung iz ye – der, ye-der, ye – der, ver es
*guard the     ghet-to gate.*     *Young is ev – 'ry-one of  us  who wants it*

vil nor,     Yo – rn ho – bn keyn ba – tayt,     Al – te
*that way*     *You're young as you want to  be.*     *Old folks*

ke – nen, ke – nen, ke – nen oykh zayn kin – der,     Fun a
*can be, must be, will be just like child – ren,*     *In a*

1. *Etc.*

nay – er, fray – er tsayt.     Ver es
*new world brave and free.*     *To ev – 'ry*

140

Fine

tsayt.
free.

Fun a nay - er fray - er tsayt.
In a new world brave and free.

| Undzer lid iz ful mit troyer,<br>Dreyst iz undzer muntergang.<br>Khotsh der soyne vakht baym toyer,<br>Shturemt yugnt mit gezang. | Our song is full of sorrow,<br>But brave is our cheerful gait.<br>With song youth will storm tomorrow,<br>Though enemies guard the ghetto gate. |
|---|---|

*Refrain*
Yung iz yeder, yeder, yeder ver
  es vil nor,
Yorn hobn keyn batayt,
Alte kenen, kenen, kenen oykh
  zayn kinder
Fun a nayer, frayer tsayt.

Refrain
*Young is every one of us who wants it
  that way,
You're young as you want to be.
Old folks can be, must be, will be just
  like children
In a new world brave and free.*

Ver es voglt um oyf vegn
Ver mit dreystkeyt s'shtelt zayn fus
Brengt di yugnt zey antkegn
Funem geto a gerus.

*To everyone with courage
Who'll take a daring stand
We young people of the ghetto
Extend a welcoming hand.*

(Refrain)

(Refrain)

Mir gedenken ale sonim.
Mir gedenken ale fraynd.
Eybik veln mir farbindn
Undzer nekhtn mitn haynt.

*We shall not forget our enemies,
We shall not forget our friends.
Our yesterdays, our tomorrows—
They are linked without an end.*

(Refrain)

(Refrain)

# ZOL SHOYN KUMEN DI GEULE

## Let Salvation Come

After the liberation, Shmerke Kaczerginski wrote a song of great significance to survivors. "Zol Shoyn Kumen di Geule" expresses the feelings of the survivor trying to make a new beginning after the Holocaust.

In addition to being physically depleted, the survivor was haunted by the conviction that life, as refracted through the memory of so much death, was worthless, as well as by guilt at having been among those who were spared. Many who found themselves the only members of their family left alive died soon after their return home.

Kaczerginski was extremely sensitive to these difficulties. After the war, he visited many camps for displaced persons, where former concentration camp inmates unwilling or unable to return to their homelands were waiting to emigrate to countries of their choice. He spoke to these people, dispensing friendship, encouragement, and advice.

Kaczerginski had a magnetism few could match. Nicknamed "Quicksilver" by virtue of his small stature and restless vivacity, he was a popular leader, fearless and full of love for life and people. During the war, before he fled the Vilna ghetto to join the partisans in the forests, he was assigned by the Germans to be part of the "paper brigade." This was a group of some twenty-five people whose job it was to sort out the most valuable sacred and scientific Jewish books for shipment to Germany. Thousands of volumes from all over Europe were thus confiscated and used by Hitler's infamous Rosenberg staff for distorted translations and anti-Semitic propaganda. German youth in particular was to be brainwashed with the falsified contents of these sacred scriptures and talmudic explanations.

While in the paper brigade at Vilna's famous Strashoun Library, which housed a precious collection of Jewish books, Kaczerginski and his co-workers managed—at constant risk of their lives—to hide many volumes. Most were buried in the grounds of the library; some were smuggled into the ghetto and hidden there.

Rachel Pupko-Melezin, a fellow member of the paper brigade, tells of Kaczerginski's daring. Once, when he came across a particularly valuable book, although it was a huge volume and he was a small man, he tucked the book under his arm and marched brazenly through the ghetto gate, singing "Young is every one of us who wants it that way" from his "Yugnt-Himen." The Germans, who liked their working brigades to sing while marching, were distracted. Unaware of the significance of the song or of the book Shmerke was carrying, they did not stop him at the ghetto gate.

The precious books salvaged by the paper brigade were retrieved after the war and brought to YIVO in New York and Yad Vashem in Jerusalem.

After the war, Kaczerginski returned from his partisan unit to his native Vilna and became the director of the government museum there. Perceiving that his main interest, the saving of Jewish books and culture, was not considered a major objective by the Vilna library authorities, he left for Lodz, where he met many of the surviving Jewish writers and poets. After the killing of survivors in the pogrom of Kielce in 1946, he and his friends left Poland for Paris. Eventually, when a job was offered to him in Buenos Aires, he moved with his wife and little daughter to Argentina. From there he traveled over Central and South America on lecture tours designed to inform people about the Holocaust. Returning from Mexico in April 1953, Kaczerginski was killed in a plane crash. He was forty-five years old. His death left a great void in the postwar generation, to which he had been of such help and inspiration.

A book in memory of Shmerke Kaczerginski, *Ondenkbukh Shmerke Kaczerginski,* was published by his friends after his death. The many tributes in the book described him with love and respect as a man with a personal philosophy formed from his knowledge of life and suffering.

Though not an intellectual, Kaczerginski had an innate sense of history and felt strongly about the importance of collecting and saving documents pertaining to the fate of the Jews during the Nazi occupation. He felt equal responsibility for the preservation of ghetto, partisan, and concentration camp songs, and made it his task to write down all those he remembered or gathered from others. He managed to have the songs published in a simple book in Warsaw, in 1947. Later that year, these songs were published by CYCO, an organization for the preservation of Jewish culture in New York, under the title *Lider fun di Getos un Lagern* (Songs of the Ghettos and Concentration Camps).

"Zol Shoyn Kumen di Geule" is set to a favorite tune of Abraham Isaac Kook, the famous mystic and chief rabbi of Jerusalem before the war. The song expresses acceptance of life and life's pleasures despite the unforgettable sufferings of the past. It is a decision in favor of optimism and joy.

# ZOL SHOYN KUMEN DI GEULE

## Let Salvation Come

Words by Shmerke Kaczerginski

Tune by Abraham Isaac Kook

On - ge - zol - yet oy - fn har - tsn, makht men a le - khay - im.___
*Though our hearts are ev - er ach - ing, to life our cups we raise.___*

Oyb der u - met lozt nit ru - en, zin - gen mir a lid.
*Though our grief will ev - er haunt us, it's life our song will praise.*

Iz ni - to keyn bi - sl bron - fn, lo - mir trin - kn may - im.___
*If there's not a drop of bran-dy, let wa - ter be our brew.___*

May - im khay - im iz dokh khay - im; vos darf nokh der Yid?
*Wa - ter, af - ter all, is life; what else___ needs a Jew?*

**Refrain A tempo**

Zol shoyn ku-men di ge - u - le,___ Zol shoyn ku-men di ge - u - le,___
*But sal - va-tion soon will come,___ Yes, sal - va-tion soon will come.___*

Zol shoyn ku-men di ge - u - le,___ Me - shi-ekh kumt shoyn bald!___
*Let Mes - si - ah___ come,___ Sal - va-tion soon will come!___*

145

Zol shoyn ku-men di ge-u – le,___ Zol shoyn ku-men di ge-u – le,___
But sal – va-tion soon will come,___ Yes, sal – va-tion soon will come,___

1. 2.

Zol shoyn ku-men di ge-u – le,___ Me – shi – ekh kumt shoyn bald!
Let Mes – si – ah___ come___ Sal – va – tion soon will come!

3.

shi – ekh kumt shoyn bald!
va – tion soon will come!

Ongezolyet oyfn hartsn, makht men a lekhayim.
Oyb der umet lozt nit ruen, zingen mir a lid.
Iz nito keyn bisl bronfn, lomir trinken mayim.
Mayim khayim iz dokh khayim—vos darf nokh der yid?

*Refrain*
Zol shoyn kumen di geule
Zol shoyn kumen di geule
Zol shoyn kumen di geule
Meshiekh kumt shoyn bald!

S'iz a dor fun kule-khayev, zayt nit keyn naronim—
Un fun zindikn—Meshiekh gikher kumen vet!
Akh, du tatele in himl, s'betn bney rakhmonim:
Ze, Meshiekh zol nit kumen a bisele tsu shpet!

*(Refrain)*

S'tantsn beymer in di velder, shtern oyfn himl.
Reb Yisroel, der mekhutn, dreyt zikh in der mit.
S'vet zikh oyfvekn Meshiekh fun zayn tifn driml
Ven er vet derhern undzer tfiledike lid.

*(Refrain)*

*Though our hearts are ever aching, to life our cups we raise.*
*Though our grief will ever haunt us, it's life our song will praise.*
*If there's not a drop of brandy, let water be our brew.*
*Water, after all, is life—what else needs a Jew?*

Refrain
*But salvation soon will come;*
*Yes, salvation soon will come.*
*Messiah soon will come.*
*Salvation soon will come.*

*We who live have not been sinless—fools deny their blame.*
*You'll see—despite all our sinning, Messiah'll come just the same!*
*Oh, hear, good Father up in heaven, your humble people's prayer:*
*That when Messiah shall arrive, some Jews will still be here!*

*(Refrain)*

*Trees are dancing in the forest, stars bright in the sky.*
*'Midst them the honored Reb Israel, twirling dances by.*
*Messiah will waken from his slumber, now he can't be long.*
*He will hurry to us when he hears our prayerful song.*

*(Refrain)*

# EPILOGUE

The slave labor camp in Peterswaldau, about 200 kilometers from Auschwitz, was liberated by Russian troops on May 9, 1945. When the camp gates opened, some eight hundred young women, pale, emaciated, dressed in rags, poured into the streets of the virtually deserted little Silesian town. It was a glorious, sunny day, the air mild and filled with the scent of blossoming trees and spring flowers in all the gardens, as if nothing had happened. We stayed in the warm sunshine for quite a while, dazed and yet ecstatic, breathing in fresh air and picking flowers from the gardens. Some of the inmates followed the Russian soldiers to German stores in town to take whatever food, clothes, and shoes they could find. They returned to the camp with bread, sugar, and other foods. Eating too much after long starvation made many sick; some even died.

In my inner world I was torn, as overwhelming joy in my regained freedom alternated with deep-seated pain and humiliation. Shame for humanity caused by the barbarism I had witnessed at such a young age was part of my state of mind.

The camp had to be dissolved within a few days, for an epidemic threatened to break out. My sister, without whom I probably would not have survived, was among those who had contracted typhus. She and other ailing camp inmates were immediately given into the care of a local hospital. Had we not been liberated at just that time, they surely would have been transferred to a death camp.

The rest of the young women departed in every direction. The Czechoslovakians were picked up by Red Cross trucks and taken to a reception camp in Nachod, a Czech town on the German border. At first I refused to leave without my sister, but when the Red Cross official promised me that I would be allowed to wait in Nachod until she got well enough to join me, I hopped on one of the last trucks and left with the others.

Nachod was a transit place for homecoming concentration camp inmates. We were examined, clothed, and fed there; those able to leave were given a nominal sum of money to travel to their hometowns. While I waited in Nachod, I helped the staff with their work and saw many hundreds of liberated prisoners arriving, most of them in pitiful condition. Their images are engraved in my mind. After several weeks, Nany joined me and we headed home.

The freight train to Galanta took three days. When we arrived, we had to face the reality that our parents, our brothers Samuel, Simon, and Ignats, and our sister Judith were not among the survivors. My brother Eugene, who had spent years in a Hungarian slave labor camp, and my oldest sister, Sophia, who was interned in Bergen-Belsen with her two small children, miraculously survived. Our house in Galanta was lived in by a strange family. Two rear rooms were vacated for us somewhat later.

We did not stay long in Czechoslovakia. Both my sisters left for Israel. My brother stayed longer; he was arrested during the 1954 purges and put in prison for six years. After his release, he settled in Western Europe. I left to study music in Switzerland.

Married to an American musician, I came to the United States in 1957. My daughter, Tamara, is a dancer.

This book was written in my New York City apartment near Riverside Park. It is a back apartment, a pleasant, quiet place in this bustling city. My bay window offers a green view of a single but leafy tree and a few shrubs—just enough to enable my imagination to go back, from time to time, to the park of my childhood, the memory of which helped to sustain me during my time in the concentration camp.

When we returned from the camp to Galanta, the park was in bad shape, neglected and trampled by the many soldiers who had passed through the town during the war and camped around the castle. Like the handful of us, the park was a survivor too. During that first summer after the war, new shoots sprouted on crumpled trees and bushes—practically in front of our eyes—and flowers bloomed even on broken branches.

A generation has grown up since that time and the number of survivors dwindles. Like the trees in the park, the songs we sang in the ghettos and concentration camps will remain to tell our stories long after we are gone. May they convey the mysterious life force that fed our will to live under those most unendurable circumstances. May they serve as life-affirming messages to present and future readers of this book.

# A GUIDE TO YIDDISH PRONUNCIATION

The Yiddish song texts in this book follow the rules of standard Yiddish formulated by YIVO (Yidisher Visnshaftlikher Institut) in Poland in 1937 in order to establish a uniform Yiddish for the linguistic community. To facilitate the reading of Yiddish texts for those unfamiliar with Hebrew letters, a consistent system of transliteration into Latin characters was established by YIVO in New York. This system has been adopted by the Library of Congress and by the academic community.

### Pronunciation Guide to Transliterated Standard Yiddish

| Vowels | Yiddish Examples | As it sounds in English |
|---|---|---|
| a | f<u>ar</u> | p<u>ar</u>t |
| e | v<u>e</u>n | wh<u>e</u>n |
| i | v<u>i</u>sn | m<u>i</u>ss |
| o | h<u>o</u>t | n<u>o</u>t |
| u | f<u>u</u>n | p<u>u</u>t |

| Diphthongs | | |
|---|---|---|
| ey | tsv<u>ey</u> | pr<u>ay</u> |
| ay | f<u>ay</u>er | f<u>i</u>re |
| oy | <u>oy</u>g | t<u>oy</u> |

**Consonants**
(if different
from the English sounds)

| | | |
|---|---|---|
| kh | i<u>kh</u> | Ba<u>ch</u> |
| g | <u>g</u>ey | <u>g</u>ive |
| dz | un<u>dz</u> | roun<u>ds</u> |
| ts | tan<u>ts</u> | fi<u>ts</u> |
| tsh | men<u>tsh</u> | pin<u>ch</u> |
| zh | shpil-<u>zh</u>e | mea<u>s</u>ure |

# ORIGINAL TEXT
# OF YIDDISH SONGS

## די נאַכט (Page 3)
## DI NAKHT

ס'איז קיינער מיט מיר אין דער נאַכט,
די נאַכט, נאָר אַליין איז מיט מיר,
אויף וועגן פֿאַרכמורעט און שטום
די שטילקייט אַליין וואַנדערט אום.
איך גיי, ס'איז אַ וויַיטער דער וועג,
פֿאַרוואָלקנט און טויב איז די נאַכט.
ווּהין פֿרעג דעם ריטעם פון טריט —
זיי גיבן קיין ענטפֿער דיר ניט.
ס'איז קיינער מיט מיר אין דער נאַכט,
די נאַכט, נאָר אַליין איז מיט מיר,
וואָס וויַיטער אַלץ וויַיטער אַהין,
ווּהין, שטילע וועגן, ווּהין?

## צווײ טײַבעלעך (Page 8)
## TSVEY TAYBELEKH

צווײ טײַבעלעך זיַינען איבערן וואַסער געפֿלויגן,
אין די פֿיסקעלעך האָבן זיי זיך געקושט.
פֿאַרשאָלטן זאָל ווערן יענער מענטש אויף דער וועלט,
וואָס ער האָס זיך אין אונדזער ליבע,
אוי, אַריַינגעמישט.

און אַז דו וועסט קומען אין אַ וויַיטן לאַנד, ליובעליו,
אין מיַינע ווערטער זאָלסטו זיך באַדענקען.
און אַז דו וועסט קומען איבער אַ טיפֿן וואַסער, ליובעליו,
פֿאַר גרויס צרות זאָלסטו זיך נישט דערטרינקען.

און אַז דו וועסט קומען אין אַ וויַיטן לאַנד, ליובעליו,
מיַינע ווערטער זאָלסטו באַקענען.
און אַז דו וועסט קומען איבער אַ גרויסן פֿיַיער, ליובעליו,
פֿאַר גרויס צרות זאָלסטו זיך נישט פֿאַרברענען.

צווײ טײַבעלעך זיַינען איבערן וואַסער געפֿלויגן,
זייערע פֿליגעלעך האָבן זיי צעשפּרייט.
פֿאַרשאָלטן זאָל ווערן יענער מענטש אויף דער וועלט,
וואָס ער האָס אונדז אין אונדזער ליבע,
אוי ווי, צעשיידעט.

## ס'ברענט (Page 13)
## S'BRENT

ס'ברענט! ברידערלעך, ס'ברענט!
אוי, אונדזער אָרעם שטעטל נעבעך ברענט!
בייזע ווינטן מיט ירגזון
רייסן, ברעכן און צעבלאָזן
שטאַרקער נאָך די ווילדע פֿלאַמען,
אַלץ אַרום שוין ברענט.

און איר שטייט און קוקט אַזוי זיך
מיט פֿאַרלייגטע הענט,
און איר שטייט און קוקט אַזוי זיך
אונדזער שטעטל ברענט!

ס'ברענט! ברידערלעך, ס'ברענט!
אוי, אונדזער אָרעם שטעטל נעבעך ברענט!
ס'האָבן שוין די פֿיַיערצונגען
דאָס גאַנצע שטעטל איַינגעשלונגען —
און די בייזע ווינטן הוזשען,
אונדזער שטעטל ברענט!

און איר שטייט און קוקט אַזוי . . .

ס'ברענט! ברידערלעך, ס'ברענט!
אוי, עס קען חלילה קומען דער מאָמענט:
אונדזער שטאָט מיט אונדז צוזאַמען,
זאָל אויף אַש אַוועק אין פֿלאַמען,
בליַיבן זאָל — ווי נאָך אַ שלאַכט,
נאָר פּוסטע, שוואַרצע וואַנט.

און איר שטייט און קוקט אַזוי זיך . . .

ס'ברענט! ברידערלעך, ס'ברענט!
די הילף איז נאָר אין איַיך אַליין געוואָנדנט.
אויב דאָס שטעטל איז איַיך טיַיר,

נעמט די כלים, לעשט דאָס פייער,
לעשט מיט אייער אייגן בלוט,
באַוויַיזט, אַז איר דאָס קענט.

שטייט נישט, ברידער, אָט אַזוי זיך
מיט פאַרלייגטע הענט,
שטייט ניט, ברידער, לעשט דאָס פייער —
אונדזער שטעטל ברענט!

## מינוטן פון בטחון (Page 18)
## MINUTN FUN BITOKHN

ייִדן, זאָל זיַין פרייליִער!
שוין ניט לאַנג, איך האָף:
ס׳עקט באַלד די מלחמה,
עס קומט באַלד זייער סוף.
פרייליִער, נאָר נטי זאָרגן
און ניט אַרומגיין טריב,
האָט גדולד, בטחון,
און נעמט אַלץ אָן פאַר ליב.

נאָר גדולד, בטחון,
ניט לאָזט אַרויס פון האַנט
אונדזער אַלט כלי-זין,
וואָס האַלט אונדז גאָר בייַנאַנד.
הוליעט, טאַנצט תלינים,
שוין ניט לאַנג, איך האָף —
געווען אַ מאָל אַ המן —
עס וואַרט אויף אים זיין סוף.

הוליעט, טאַנצט תלינים,
לייַדן קען אַ ייִד,
ס׳וועט די שווערסטע אַרבעט
אונדז קיין מאָל מאַכן מיד.
קערן? זאָל זיין קערן!
כל-זמן איר וועט זיַין,
איז אומזיסט דאָס קערן,
ס׳וועט דאָ ניט ווערן ריַין.

וואַשן? זאָל זיַין וואַשן!
קיינס רויטער פלעק,
האַבלס בלוט פון האַרצן —
דאָס וואַשט זיך ניט אַוועק.
טריַיבט אונדז פון די דירות,
שנייַדט אונדז אָפ די בערד!
ייִדן, זאָל זיַין פרייליִער! —
מיר האַבן זיי אין דר׳ערד!

## באַבי-יאַר (Page 23)   BABI YAR

וואָלט איך אויפגעהאַנגען
דאָס וויגל אויף אַ באַלקן
און געהוידעט, געהוידעט
מייַן ייִנגעלע, מייַן יאַנקל.
איז די שטוב אַנטרונענען
מיט אַ פלאַם פייַער
ווי זשע קאָן איך הוידען
מייַן ייִנגעלע, מייַן טייַערן?

. . . אַ

וואָלט איך אויפגעהאַנגען
דאָס וויגל אויף אַ ביימל,
און געהוידעט, געהוידעט,
מייַן ייִנגעלע, מייַן שליימל,
איז מיר ניט געבליבן
קיין פאָדעם פון קיין ציך,
איז מיר ניט געבליבן
קיין בענדל פון קיין שיך.

. . . אַ

וואָלט איך אָפגעשאָרן
די צעפ מייַנע, די לאַנגע,
און אויף זיי דאָס וויגל,
דאָס וויגל אויפגעהאַנגען,
ווייס איך ניט, וווּ זוכט מען
די ביינדעלער אַצינדער,
די ביינדעלער, די טייַערע,
פון ביידע מייַנע קינדער.

. . . אַ

העלפט מיר, מאַמעס, העלפט מיר
אויסקלאָגן מיין ניגון,
העלפט מיר, מאַמעס, העלפט מיר
דעם באַבי-יאַר פאַרוויגן.

. . . אַ    ליולינקע-ליו-ליו . . .

## צען ברידער (Page 48)   TSEN BRIDER

צען ברידער זענען מיר געווען
האָבן מיר געהאַנדלט מיט וויַין,
איינער איז געשטאָרבן,
זענען מיר געבליבן ניַין.
אַי, אַי, אַי, אַי.

ייִדל מיטן פֿידל, משה מיטן באַס,
שפילט זשע מיר אַ לידל,
מע פירט אונדז צו דעם גאַז.

נאָר אויב פֿאַרזאַמען וועט די זון אין דעם קאַיאָר,
ווי אַ פּאַראָל זאָל גיין דאָס ליד פֿון דור צו דור!

געשריבן איז דאָס ליד מיט בלוט און ניט מיט בלײַ.
ס׳איז ניט קיין לידל פֿון אַ פֿויגל אויף דער פֿרײַ —
דאָס האָט אַ פֿאָלק צעווישן פֿאַלנדיקע ווענט
דאָס ליד געזונגען מיט נאַגאַנעס אין די הענט.

טאָ זאָג ניט קיין מאָל, אַז דו גייסט דעם לעצטן וועג,
ווען הימלען בלייענע פֿאַרשטעלן בלאָע טעג.
קומען וועט נאָך אונדזער אויסגעבענקטע שעה,
עס וועט אַ פּויק טאָן אונדזער טראָט: "מיר זײַנען דאָ!"

# שטיל, די נאַכט איז אויסגעשטערנט
## (Page 70)
## SHTIL , DI NAKHT IZ OYSGESHTERNT

שטיל, די נאַכט איז אויסגעשטערנט,
און דער פֿראָסט — ער האָט געברענט;
צי געדענקסטו ווי איך האָב דיך געלערנט
האַלטן אַ שפּײַער אין די הענט.

אַ מויד, אַ פּעלצל און אַ בערעט,
און האַלט אין האַנט פֿעסט אַ נאַגאַן,
אַ מויד מיט אַ סאַמעטענעם פּנים
היט אָפּ דעם שׂונעס קאַראָוואַן.

געצילט, געשאָסן און געטראָפֿן
האָט איר קליינינקער פּיסטויל,
אַן אויטאָ אַ פֿולינק מיט וואָפֿן
פֿאַרהאַלטן האָט זי מיט אַיין קויל.

פֿאַר טאָג פֿון וואַלד אַרויסגעקראָכן,
מיט שניי-גירלאַנדן אויף די האָר,
געמוטיקט פֿון קליינינקן נצחון
פֿאַר אונדזער נײַעם, פֿרײַען דור.

# יעדער רופֿט מיך זיאַמעלע
## ZIAMELE (Page 76)

יעדער רופֿט מיך זיאַמעלע,
אַי, ווי מיר איז שווער.
כ׳האָב געהאַט אַ מאַמעלע,
כ׳האָב זי שוין ניט מער.
כ׳האָב געהאַט אַ טאַטעלע,
האָט ער מיך געהיט.
איצט בין איך אַ שמאַטעלע,
ווײַל איך בין אַ ייִד.

כ׳האָב געהאַט אַ שוועסטערל,
איז זי מער נישטאָ.
אוי, ווי ביסטו אסתרל,
איז דער שווערער שעה?

אײַן ברודער נאָר בין איך מיר געבליבן,
מיט וועמען זאָל איך וויינען?
די אַנדערע נײַן האָט מען דערהרגעט,
צי געדענקט ווער זייערע נעמען?

ייִדל מיטן פידל, משה מיטן באַס,
הערט מײַן לעצטע לידל,
מע פירט מיך אויף צום גאַז.

צען ברידער זענען מיר געווען
מיר האָבן קיינעם ניט ווײ געטאָן.

# וואַרשע VARSHE (Page 58)

ס׳פֿאַרשווינדט ניט די נאַכט און דער טאָג קומט ניט אָן,
אַ בלוטיקע קויל ווערט די ערד שוין.
אַ ייִד פֿלאַטערט אויף ווי אַ שטורמישע פֿאָן,
אַ פֿאָן אינעם טאָל פֿון די מתים.

אין חורבֿות דאָס געטאָ, די ייִדן — אין שלאַכט,
דער ייִד שפּרײַזט דורך רויך און דורך פֿלאַמען,
— נקמה! נקמה! — ער שטורעמט די נאַכט,
פֿאַר קינדער, פֿאַר טאַטעס, פֿאַר מאַמעס!

דער שׂנאי שיט און שיט און די ערד ווערט ניט ווײַס,
עס האַלט נאָך דאָס בלוט אין אײן זידן,
עס רופֿט נאָך נקמה אויף שנײַיִקן אײַז,
— דאָס בלוט פֿון די העלדישע ייִדן.

קיין טאָג וועט ניט זײַן, — רופֿט דער ייִד — און קיין נאַכט,
מיר וועלן דער וועלט ניט פֿאַרגעבן!
די וועלכע זײַנען געפֿאַלן אין שלאַכט,
אייביק אין אונדז וועלן לעבן!

מיר וועלן געדענקען דעם ווײ און דעם מוט,
עס פֿיבערט אין גלי די נשמה,
קריץ אויס זיך אין האַרצן דרײַ ווערטער פֿון בלוט:
נקמה! נקמה! נקמה!

# פּאַרטיזאַנער-הימען (Page 64)
## ZOG NIT KEYNMOL

זאָג ניט קיין מאָל, אַז דו גייסט דעם לעצטן וועג,
ווען הימלען בלייענע פֿאַרשטעלן בלאָע טעג.
קומען וועט נאָך אונדזער אויסגעבענקטע שעה,
עס וועט אַ פּויק טאָן אונדזער טראָט: "מיר זײַנען דאָ!"

פֿון גרינעם פּאַלמענלאַנד ביז לאַנד פֿון ווײַסן שניי
מיר קומען אָן מיט אונדזער פּײַן, מיט אונדזער ווי,
און ווו געפֿאַלן איז אַ שפּריץ פֿון אונדזער בלוט,
שפּראָצן וועט דאָרט אונדזער גבֿורה, אונדזער מוט.

עס וועט די מאָרגנזון באַגילדן אונדז דעם הײַנט,
און דער נעכטן וועט פֿאַרשווינדן מיטן פֿײַנד.

153

ערגעץ ביַי אַ ביימעלע,
ערגעץ ביַי אַ פלוט,
ליגט מיַין ברודער שלמהלע,
פֿון אַ דייַטש געטויט.

כ'האָב געהאַט אַ היימעלע,
איצט איז מיר שלעכט,
כ'בין ווי אַ בהמהלע,
וואָס דער תליון שעכט.
אַך דו גאָט אין הימעלע,
קוק אויף דער ערד אַראָפּ,
זע נאָר ווי דייַן בלימעלע,
שניַידט דער תליון אָפּ.

## רבֿקהלע די שבתדיקע (Page 81)

### RIFKELE, DI SHABESDIKE

רבֿקהלע די שבתדיקע
אַרבעט אין פֿאַבריק,
דרייט אַ פֿאָדעם צו אַ פֿאָדעם,
פֿלעכט צונויף אַ שטריק.
אוי, די געטאָ פֿינצטערע,
דויערט שוין צו לאַנג,
און דאָס האַרץ אַזוי פֿאַרקלעמט
טוט איר אַזוי באַנג.

איר געטרייַער הערשעלע
איז אַוועק, ניטאָ,
זינט פֿון יענעם שבת אָן,
זינט פֿון יענער שעה.
איז פֿאַרטרויערט רבֿקהלע,
יאָמערט טאָג און נאַכט,
און אַצינד ביַים רעדעלע,
זיצט זי און זי טראַכט.

ווו איז ער, מיַין ליבינקער,
לעבט ער נאָך כאָטש ווו?
צי אין קאָנצענטראַציע-לאַגער
אַרבעט שווער אָן רו?
אוי, ווי פֿינצטער איז אים דאָרט,
ביטער איז מיר דאָ —
זינט פֿון יענעם שבת אָן,
זינט פֿון יענער שעה.

## ציגייַנער-ליד (Page 87)

### TSIGAYNERLID

פֿינצטער די נאַכט
ווי קוילן שוואַרץ, —
נאָר כ'טראַכט און טראַכט
און ס'קלאַפֿט מיַין האַרץ:
מיר, ציגייַנער, לעבן ווי קיינער,
מיר ליַידן נויט,
גענוג קוים אויף ברויט.

דזום, דזום, דזום, דזום, דזום, דזום, דזום,
מיר פליען אַרום ווי די טשייַקעס.
דזום, דזום, דזום, דזום, דזום, דזום, דזום,
און מיר שפילן אויף די באַלאַלייַקעס.

ניט ווּאָ מען טאָגט,
ניט ווּאָ מען נאַכט,
יעדער זיך פּלאָגט,
נאָר כ'טראַכט און טראַכט:
מיר, ציגייַנער, לעבן ווי קיינער,
מיר ליַידן נויט,
גענוג קוים אויף ברויט.

דזום, דזום, דזום, דזום . . .

## אין קרייּוווקע (Page 101)

### IN KRIUVKE

איך זיץ אין קרייּוווקע און איך טראַכט זיך:
איך בין שוין מיד אַז דאָס אויג פֿאַרמאַכט זיך,
איך בין געבליבן אַליין, איך באַגיס זיך מיט געוויין —
צי וועלן מיר פֿון דאַנען אַרויסגיין?

שפילט, שפילט, סטרונעס פֿון פּיַין,
שפילט זשע מיר אַ ייִדישן ניגון.
שפילט, שפילט, סטרונעס פֿון פּיַין,
צי וועלן מיר דערלעבן דעם פֿריידן.

מיר זיַינען אַ פֿאָלק מיט מוחות,
פֿון צרות האָבן מיר שוין ניט קיין כוחות,
יעדן פֿאָלק איז גוט; עס גיסט זיך ייִדיש בלוט —
אוי, העלף אונדז, גאָט, אין איצטיקער מינוט.

שפילט, שפילט . . .

פֿאַר דעם קריג האָבן מיר געלעבט אין פֿריידן,
איז געקומען היטלער און אויסגעמאָרדעט אַלע ייִדן.
געוועוזן זיַינען מיר רויִק, מיט אַלע פֿעלקער גליַיך,
אין וואָס באַשטייט אונדזער זינד, פֿרעג איך ביַי אייַך?

שפילט, שפילט . . .

איך האָב געלעבט אין האָפֿענונג, אין שטרעבן,
איך בין נאָך יונג, עס ווילט זיך מיר נאָר לעבן.
געוועוזן בין איך קליין, ביַי מיַין מאַמען אין דער היים —
און היינט בין איך אַ באַנדיט אין וואַלד אַליין.

שפילט, שפילט . . .

## טרעבלינקע (Page 106)

### TREBLINKE

דאָרט, ניט וויַיט פֿון דאַרף,
דאָרט איז דער אומשלאַגפּלאַץ געלייגט.
דאָרט ווו מע שטופּט זיך אין דער ברייט
אין די וואַגאָנען אַריַין.
און דאָרטן הערט מען אַ געשריַי

ווי אײַן קינד וויינט צו דער מאַמען:
געלאָזט האָסטו מיר גאַנץ אַליין,
כ׳וויל בלײַבן מיט דיר צוזאַמען.

די ייִדישע פּאָליציי,
זי האָט געהייסן שנעלער גיין,
"איר וועט ניט וויסן פֿון קיין נויט
איר וועט באַקומען צו עסן ברויט".
און אזוי האָבן זיי אונדז פֿאַרנאַרט.
אז מיר וועלן באַקומען צו עסן ברויט,
און קיינער פֿון אונדז האָט ניט געגלויבט
אין טרעבלינקע דעם שנעלן טויט.

קום צוריק, צוריק, מײַן מאַמעניו.
קום, אך קום, צוריק צו מיר.
קום צוריק, צוריק, מײַן מאַמעניו.
די גאַנצע צײַט בין איך געווען מיט דיר.

טרעבלינקע דאָרף,
פֿון אלע ייִדן גוטער אָרט.
ווער ס׳קומט אהין דער בלייבט שוין דאָרט.
דער בלייבט אויף אייביק דאָרט.
ווער ס׳קומט אהין,
פֿון ברידער, שוועסטער, טאַטעס, מאַמעס,
און דאָרטן טוט מען זיי פֿאַרצאַמען
און דאָרט איז זייער סוף.

# שטילער, שטילער (Page 114)
## SHTILER, SHTILER

שטילער, שטילער, לאָמיר שווײַגן,
קבֿרים וואַקסן דאָ.
ס׳האָבן זיי פֿאַרפֿלאַנצט די שונאים;
גרינען זיי צום בלאָ.
ס׳פֿירען וועגן צו פֿאַנאַר צו,
ס׳פֿירט קיין וועג צוריק,
איז דיר טאַטע וווּ פֿאַרשוווּנדן,
און מיט אים דאָס גליק.
שטילער, קינד מײַנס, וויין ניט, אוצר,
ס׳העלפֿט ניט קיין געוויין,
אונדזער אומגליק וועלן שונאים
סײַ-ווי ניט פֿאַרשטיין.
ס׳האָבן ברעגעס אויך די ימען,
ס׳האָבן תּפֿיסות אויכעט צאַמען,
נאָר צו אונדזער פּײַן
קיין ביסל שײַן,
קיין ביסל שײַן.

פֿרילינג אויפֿן לאַנד געקומען, —
און אונדז האַרבסט געבראַכט,
איז דער טאָג הײַנט פֿול מיט בלומען, —
אונדז זעט נאָר די נאַכט.
גאָלדיקט שוין דער האַרבסט אויף שטאַמען, —
בליט אין אונדז דער צער;

בלײַבט פֿאַריתומט ווי אַ מאַמע;
ס׳קינד גייט אויף פֿאַנאַר.
ווי די וויליע אַ געשמידטע —
ט׳אויך גע...אקט אין פּײַן, —
ציִען קריעס אײַן דורך ליטע
איצט אין ים אַרײַן.
ס׳ווערט דער חושך ווי צערונען,
פֿון דער פֿינצטער לײַכטן זונען —
רײַטער, קום געשווינד, —
דיך רופֿט דײַן קינד,
דיק רופֿט דײַן קינד.

שטילער, שטילער, ס׳קוועלן קוואַלן
אונדז אין האַרץ אַרום,
ביז דער טויער וועט ניט פֿאַלן
זײַן מיר מוזן שטום.
פֿרײַ ניט, קינד, זיך, ס׳איז דײַן שמייכל
איצט פֿאַר אונדז פֿאַרראַט,
זען דעם פֿרילינג זאָל דער שׂונא
ווי אין האַרבסט אַ בלאַט.
זאָל דער קוואַל זיך רויִק פֿליסן,
שטילער זײַ און האָף . . .
מיט דער פֿרײַהײט קומט דער טאַטע,
שלאָף זשע, קינד מײַן, שלאָף.
ווי די וויליע אַ באַפֿרײַטע,
ווי די ביימער גרין-באַנײַטע
לײַכט באַלד פֿרײַהייטס-ליכט
אויף דײַן געזיכט,
אויף דײַן געזיכט.

# דרעמלען פֿייגל אויף די צווייגן
## DREMLEN FEYGL (Page 120)

דרעמלען פֿייגל אויף די צווייגן,
שלאָף, מײַן טײַער קינד.
בײַ דײַן וויגל אויף דײַן נאַרע
זיצט אַ פֿרעמדע און זינגט:
ליו-ליו, ליו-ליו, ליו.

ס׳איז דײַן וויגל וווּ געשטאַנען
אויסגעפֿלאָכטן פֿון גליק,
און דײַן מאַמע, אױ דײַן מאַמע
קומט שוין קיין מאָל ניט צוריק.
ליו-ליו, ליו-ליו, ליו.

כ׳האָב געזען דײַן טאַטן לויפֿן
אונטער האָגל פֿון שטיין,
איבער פֿעלדער איז געפֿלויגן
זײַן פֿאַריתומטער געוויין.
ליו-ליו, ליו-ליו, ליו.

## ישראליק YISROLIK (Page 124)

נו, קױפֿט זשע פּאַפּיראָסן,
נו, קױפֿט זשע סאַכאַרין,
געװאָרן איז הײַנט סחורה ביליק װערט.
אַ לעבן פֿאַר אַ גראָשן
אַ פּרוטה — אַ פֿאַרדינסט —
פֿון געטאָ-הענדלער האָט איר דאָך געהערט.

(צוזינג:)

כ׳הייס ישראליק
איך בין דאָס קינד פֿון געטאָ,
כ׳הייס ישראליק
אַ הפֿקרדיקער יונג.
כאַטש פֿאַרבליבן גאָלע נעטאָ
דערלאַנג איך אַלץ נאָך
אַ סװישטשע און אַ זונג!

אַ מאַנטל אָן אַ קראַגן,
תחתונים פֿון אַ זאַק,
קאַלאָשן האָב איך, — ס׳פֿעלן נאָר די שיך.
און װער עס װעט נאָר װאָגן
צו לאַכן, אױ, אַ סך —
דעם װעל איך נאָך װײַזן װער בין איך!

כ׳הייס ישראליק . . .

ניט מײַנט, מיך האָט געבאָרן
די הפֿקרדיקע גאַס —
בײַ טאַטע-מאַמע אױך געװען אַ קינד.
כ׳האָב בײדן אָנגעװאָרן,
ניט מײַנט עס איז אַ שפּאַס,
כ׳בין געבליבן, װי אין פֿעלד דער װינט.

כ׳הייס ישראליק,
נאָר װען קיינער זעט ניט,
װיש איך שטיל זיך
פֿון אױג אַראָפּ אַ טרער —
נאָר פֿון מײַן טרױער —
בעסער אַז מע רעדט ניט,
צו װאָס דערמאָנען
און מאַכן ס׳האַרץ זיך שװער.

## האָט זיך מיר די שיך צעריסן
TANTS, TANTS, TANTS (Page 130)

האָט זיך מיר די שיך צעריסן,
װיי צו מײַנע יאָרן,
די קראָגנס האָט מען אונדז אָפּגעריסן —
װער איך דאָך פֿאַרפֿראָרן.
טאַנץ, טאַנץ, טאַנץ אַ ביסעלע מיט מיר,
אױ איר גרױסע פֿרעסטעלעך,
איר קומט דאָך פֿון סיביר.

---

געלע שײַנען, ראָזע שײַנען,
אַלערליי קאָלירן.
װען װעל איז מײַן װײַבל זלאַטע
צו זיך אַהיים שױן פֿירן?
טאַנץ, טאַנץ, טאַנץ אַ ביסעלע מיט מיר,
האָסטו אַ געלן שײַן,
האָב איך חתונה מיט דיר.

ברױט אױפֿן סענטימעטער,
האָלץ אױפֿן דעקאַ,
האָט אונדז פֿאַרזאָרגט דער ייִדנראַט,
דער ייִדנראַט פֿון געטאָ,
טאַנץ, טאַנץ, טאַנץ אַ ביסעלע מיט מיר,
האָסטו אַ געלן שײַן,
האָב איך חתונה מיט דיר.

## יוגנט־הימען YUGNT-HIMEN (Page 137)

אונדזער ליד איז פֿול מיט טרױער, —
דרייסט איז אונדזער מונטערגאַנג,
כאַטש דער שונא װאַכט בײַם טױער, —
שטורעמט יוגנט מיט געזאַנג:

יונג איז יעדער, יעדער, יעדער װער עס װיל נאָר,
יאָרן האָבן קיין באַטײַט,
אַלטע קענען, קענען, קענען אױך זײַן קינדער
פֿון אַ נײַער פֿרײַער צײַט.

װער עס װאָגלט אום אױף װעגן,
װער מיט דרייסטקייט ס׳שטעלט זײַן פֿוס,
ברענגט די יוגנט זיי אַנטקעגן
פֿונעם געטאָ אַ גערוס.

יונג איז יעדער . . .

מיר געדענקען אַלע שונאים,
מיר געדענקען אַלע פֿרײַנד,
אייביק װעלן מיר דערמאָנען,
אונדזער נעכטן מיטן הײַנט.

יונג איז יעדער . . .

קלױבן מיר צונױף די גלידער,
װידער שטאָלן מיר די רייַ.
גייט אַ בױער, גייט אַ שמידער, —
לאָמיר אַלע גיין מיט זיי!

יונג איז יעדער . . .

# זאָל שוין קומען די גאולה

## ZOL SHOYN KUMEN DI GEULE  (Page 142)

אָנגעזאַליעט אויפֿן האַרצן, מאַכט מען אַ לחיים,
אייב דער אומעט לאָזט ניט רוען — זינגען מיר אַ ליד.
איז ניטאָ קיין ביסל בראָנפֿן — לאָמיר טרינקען מים,
מים־חיים איז דאָך חיים — וואָס דאַרף נאָך אַ ייד?

זאָל שוין קומען די גאולה,
משיח קומט שוין באַלד!

ס׳איז אַ דור פֿון כולו חייב, זײַט ניט קיין נאַראָנים —
אין פֿון זינדיקן — משיח גיכער קומען וועט?
אָך, דו טאַטעלע אין הימל, ס׳בעטן בני רחמנים:
זע, משיח זאָל ניט קומען אַ ביסעלע צו שפּעט . . .

זאָל שוין קומען די גאולה,
משיח קומט שוין באַלד!

ס׳טאָנצן ביימער אין די וועלדער, שטערן אויפֿן הימל,
ר׳ ישראל, דיר מחותן, דרייט זיך אין דער מיט,
ס׳וועט זיך אויפֿוועקן משיח פֿון זײַן טיפֿן דרימל
ווען ער וועט דערהערן אונדזער תּפֿילהדיקע ליד.

זאָל שוין קומען די גאולה,
משיח קומט שוין באַלד!

# BIBLIOGRAPHY

Arad, Yitzhak. *Ghetto in Flames.* Yad Vashem, Jerusalem: Antidefamation League, 1980.

———. *The Partisan.* New York: Holocaust Library, Schocken Books, 1979.

Baker, Leonard. *Days of Sorrow and Pain.* New York: Macmillan, 1978.

Bauer, Yehuda. *The Holocaust in Human Perspective.* Seattle: University of Washington Press, 1978.

Biss, André. *A Million Jews to Save: Check to the Final Solution.* London: Hutchinson, 1966.

*The Black Book:* The Nazi Crime Against the Jewish People. New York: The Jewish Black Book Committee, 1946.

Braham, Randolph L. *The Politics of Genocide.* New York: Columbia University Press, 1981.

Dawidowicz, Lucy S. *The Holocaust Reader.* Library of Jewish Studies. New York: Behrman House, 1976.

———. *The War Against the Jews.* New York: Holt, Rinehart & Winston, 1975.

Des Pres, Terrence. *The Survivor.* New York: Oxford University Press, 1976.

Donat, Alexander, ed. *The Death Camp Treblinka.* New York: Holocaust Library, Schocken Books, 1979.

Dworecki, Mark. *Hirshke Glick.* Paris, 1966.

———. *Yerushalayim D'Lita in Kampf u. Umkum.* Paris: Yidisher Natsionaler Arbeter Farband, 1948.

Eckman, Lester, and Lazar, Chaim. *The Jewish Resistance.* New York: Shengold Publishers, 1977.

Eisenberg, Azriel. *Witness to the Holocaust.* New York: The Pilgrim Press, 1981.

Fater, Yisaskhar. *Yidishe Muzik in Polyn.* Tel Aviv: Veltfederatsie fun Poylishe Yidn, 1970.

Friedman, Philip. *Martyrs and Fighters.* New York: Praeger, 1954.

Galili-Gemeiner, Ervin. *Tanu'k Vagyunk.* Tel Aviv, 1969.

Goes, Albrecht. *The Burnt Offering.* New York: Pantheon, 1956.

Hilberg, Raul. *The Destruction of the European Jews.* Rev. ed. New York: Holmes and Meier, 1984.

Hirshaut, Julien. *Jewish Martyrs of Pawiak.* New York: Holocaust Library, 1982.

Kaczerginski, Shmerke. *Khurbn Vilne.* New York: CYCO Bikher Farlag, 1946.

Kantor, Alfred. *The Book of Alfred Kantor.* New York: McGraw-Hill, 1971.

Kaplan, Joseph, ed. *Fun Letstn Khurbn.* Munich, 1946–47.

Kenrick, Donald. *The Destiny of Europe's Gypsies.* London: Sussex University Press, 1972.

Klarsfeld, Beate. *Wherever They May Be!* New York: Vanguard Press, 1975.

Kogon, Eugen. *The Theory and Practice of Hell.* New York: Farrar, Straus and Cudahy, 1950.

Kren, George M., and Rappoport, Leon. *The Holocaust and the Crisis of Human Behavior.* New York: Holmes and Meier, 1980.

Kruk, Herman. *Togbukh fun Vilner Geto.* New York: Yivo Institute, 1961.

Langbein, Hermann. *Im Namen de Deutschen Volkes.* Vienna: Europa Verlag, 1963.

———. *Menschen in Auschwitz.* Vienna: Europa Verlag, 1972.

Levi, Primo. *Survival in Auschwitz.* New York: Collier Books, 1961.

Levin, Nora. *Holocaust: The Destruction of European Jewry, 1933–1945.* New York: T. Y. Crowell, 1968.

Mead, Vladka. *On Both Sides of the Wall.* Israel: Ghetto Fighters' House, Publishers, 1973.

Meltzer, Milton. *Never to Forget.* New York: Harper & Row, 1976.

*Mezritsh Zamlbukh.* Buenos Aires, 1952.

Morse, Arthur D. *While Six Millions Died.* New York: Random House, 1968.

*Ondenbukh Shmerke Kaczerginski.* Buenos Aires: Special Committee for Shmerke Kaczerginski, 1955.

Poliakov, Leon. *Harvest of Hate.* New York: Holocaust Library, Schocken Books, 1979.

Rabinowicz, Harry M. *The Legacy of Polish Jewry.* New York: Thomas Yoseloff, 1965.

Reitlinger, Gerald. *The Final Solution.* New York: A. S. Barnes, 1953.

Reynolds, Quentin et al. *Minister of Death.* New York: Viking Press, 1960.

Ringelblum, Emanuel. *Notes from the Warsaw Ghetto.* Translated from the Yiddish by Jacob Sloan. New York: Schocken, 1958.

Rolnik, Masha. *Ikh Muz Dertseyln.* Warsaw: Yidish Bukh Farlag, 1965.

Rubenstein, Richard J. *After Auschwitz.* Indianapolis: Bobbs-Merrill, 1966.

Rudashovsky, Yitskhok. *The Diary of the Vilna Ghetto.* Israel: Ghetto Fighters' Publishing House, 1973.

Russel, Lord of Liverpool. *The Scourge of the Swastika.* New York: Philosophical Library, 1954.

Schwartz, Leo Walder. *The Root and the Bough.* New York: Rinehart, 1948.

Stadtler, Bea. *The Holocaust: A History of Courage and Resistance.* New York: Behrman House, 1974.

Steinmetz, Selma. *Osterreich's Zigeuner im NS-Staat.* Vienna: Europa Verlag, 1966.

Sutskever, A. *Vilner Geto.* Paris: Farband fun di Vilner in Frankraykh, 1946.

Syrkin, Marie. *Blessed Is the Match.* New York: Knopf, 1949.

Tannenbaum, I. *Tsvishn Milkhome un Sholem.* Buenos Aires: Tsentral-Ferband fun Poylishe Yidn, 1956.

Trunk, Isaiah. *Jewish Responses to Nazi Persecution.* New York: Stein & Day, 1978.

Turkow, Jonas. *Farloshene Shtern.* Buenos Aires: Farband fun Poylishe Yidn in Argentine, 1953.

Turkow, Zigmunt. *Di Ibergerisene T'kufe.* Buenos Aires: Farband fun Poylishe Yidn in Argentine, 1961.

Tushnet, Leonard. *The Pavement of Hell.* New York: St. Martin's Press, 1972.

Weiss, Peter. *Die Ermittlung.* Frankfurt: Suhrkamp Verlag, 1956.

Wiesel, Elie. *Legends of Our Time.* New York: Holt, Rinehart & Winston, 1968.

———. *Night.* New York: Hill and Wang, 1961.

Yerushalmi, Elieser. *Das Jüdische Martyrerkind.* Darmstadt: Ökumenische Marienschwesternschaft, 1960.

Yoors, Jan. *Crossing.* New York: Simon & Schuster, 1971.

Ziemian, Joseph. *The Cigarette Sellers of the Three Crosses Square.* London: Valentine Mitchell, 1970.

Zylbercweig, Zalmen. *Lexicon of the Yiddish Theatre.* Mexico City: 1967.